Augsburg
Sermons for
Children

Gospels, Series B

Augsburg
Sermons for
Children

Augsburg
MINNEAPOLIS

AUGSBURG SERMONS FOR CHILDREN
Gospels, Series B

Interior design: Virginia Aretz, Northwestern Printcrafters
Cover design: Lecy Design

Library of Congress Cataloging-in-Publication Data

Augsburg sermons for children
    p. cm.
   Contents: [1] Series A — [2] Series B.
   1. Bible. N.T. Gospels—Children's sermons.
  2. Lutheran Church—Sermons. 3. Church Year sermons.
  4. Sermons, American. I. Augsburg Fortress (Publisher)
  BS2555.4.A945 1992   252′.53   92-27959
  ISBN 0-8066-2621-6 (pbk. : v. 1 : alk. paper)
  ISBN 0-8066-2622-4 (pbk. : v. 2 : alk. paper)

                                                 92-27959
                                                 CIP

Manufactured in the U.S.A.   AF 9-2622

5   6   7   8   9   10

NOTE * Based on the Common Lectionary (CL)

Contents

———————————————•———————————————

Susan K. Liberati, Teacher
Forest Hill, Maryland

Lori Rosenkvist, Writer
Tofte, Minnesota

Preface

————————————•————————————

When the disciples of Jesus tried to prevent parents from bringing their children to him, Jesus stopped the disciples and told them to let the children come to him; he included children in his ministry.

Sometimes the church has done little to include children in its worship services. Now many pastors and church leaders are exploring a number of ways for children to participate, and the children's sermon has great potential.[1] During this special time, the gospel can be communicated to children in ways particularly appropriate for them, taking seriously children's concerns, level of understanding, and interests. Children are full members in the household of faith, and nothing is more important than sowing the seeds of the gospel early in life.

The goal of this book is to present children's sermons through which children can begin to realize the immensity of God's love for them and God's acceptance of them as they are. Even though the messages and activities use simple language and basic concepts, the gospel is not trivialized. The writers of these children's sermons hope that the children will experience God's love and feel the joy that such good news brings.

The introductory material for each sermon provides helpful information for those using this book. After the Sunday and Gospel text, there are three headings: Focus, Experience, and Preparation. The focus statement encapsulates the theme, the experience statement tells what activity is planned, and the preparations statement describes what needs to be done ahead of time. Though adaptations can be made, these keys for effective use provide basic information about the authors' intentions.

Because "doing" is as important as "talking" with children, the children's sermons in this book are designed to encourage active participation as well as conversation with the children. The emphasis is on all levels of being: not just what to think about (the intel-

———————————

1. *Including Children in Worship* by Elizabeth J. Sandell is an excellent resource that gives many practical ideas beyond children's sermons (Augsburg, Minneapolis).

lectual) but also their feelings about relationships, experiences, and discoveries (the affective).

Some of the children's sermons begin with the use of props, objects, or special arrangements, but these sermons are not like some object lessons that ask children to make symbolic connections between an object and a spiritual concept. Such abstract thinking is beyond most children's ability. Objects and props in these sermons are from the children's own experiences and the concepts are on a level they can understand.

If an object or a prop is part of a children's sermon, let the children hold it and handle it when that is possible. They will learn more from their own experience than from simply watching you. Asking a couple of children to help you open the backpack or hold the posterboard helps them feel needed and important.

As you plan to present these children's sermons, you will bring your own style and gifts to your time with the children. Your gifts of spontaneity, flexibility, and creativity will give life to the messages. Children are usually eager to join in the experiences you lead, and your enthusiasm will help them gain much from your time together.

Your primary audience will be the children who come forward to participate, but other children too hesitant or shy to come up, as well as adults and youth, will also be listening and watching. When you ask the children questions, all the people in the congregation will be listening and probably answering to themselves.

The congregation may respond to the dialogue that is part of the children's sermon with warm, affirming laughter. This is usually not disruptive but rather extends the dialogue and lets you know the congregation is listening. There can be a temptation to play to this larger audience, but do not give in to it. The children will sense that they are no longer your primary focus, and you will break the essential bond you have been developing with them.

Effective dialogue develops with good questions and responses. Open questions, such as "What do you do when you know a storm is coming?", generate interesting responses. Because you do not suggest a particular answer, you are more likely to get authentic and sometimes unexpected responses. Closed questions, ones that can be answered with yes or no or a brief, factual answer rarely lead to further conversation. Yet some closed questions are helpful to define words or identify a person or action. For example, "What was Jesus doing when the storm came up?" (Luke 8:22-25) can be answered, "He was sleeping." Following that with open questions will involve the children more fully.

Children's sermons that are more grace oriented than law oriented convey God's love more clearly. As much as possible, messages to children should communicate how God shows grace through Jesus Christ; how God has worked through the lives of people in Bible times, throughout the ages, and today; and how God loves each one of them very much.[2]

---

2. Special thanks to Lisa Stafford and Gail Wettstein, contributors to *Augsburg Sermons for Children, Gospels, Series A,* who provided some of the material used in this preface.

First Sunday in Advent

————————————————— • —————————————————

The Gospel: Mark 13:33-37

Focus: Jesus told his followers to watch and be ready for his return.

Experience: A simple test will show the children how hard it is to be ready, even for something that's expected.

Preparation: Bring a wooden yardstick.

Ready or Not . . .

We're going to try an experiment today. Could I have a volunteer to help me? (*Pick an older child.*) OK, (*child's name*), I'm going to test you to see how alert you are. (*Hold the yardstick vertically by the 36" end, with the 1" mark at the bottom. Hold it high enough that the child can comfortably put his or her hands on either side of the yardstick at the 1" mark. Position the child's hands as directed.*) I'm going to drop the yardstick. You will catch it. If you're really alert, it won't fall very far before you grab it. I'll see how many inches have gone by, and that will tell me how you did. Are you ready? One—two—three—go! (*Drop the stick. Note what number is just above the child's hands.*) Good for you! Let's try a second time and see if you do even better.

(*Hold the yardstick up again. This time, however, drop it without warning as you address comments to the group.*) Ready, (*name*)? Maybe the rest of you think this looks easy, but it takes concentration. What do you think? Will (*name*) do better the second time? It takes quick hands and quick reaction time. (*Drop the stick on the first "quick".*)

All right, (*name*), was it harder the first time or the second time? (*Child will probably say the second time.*) Did it help when I warned you before I let go? (*Probably yes.*) Well, even when I didn't warn you, you knew your job was to be ready to catch the yardstick. But it's hard to be alert all the time, isn't it?

In today's Scripture, Jesus told his followers that he would come back to earth one day, but he said that no one except God knows when that will happen—the time of day or the season or even the year this will happen. But just as (*name*) had to be ready for me to drop the yardstick, we are to watch and wait for Jesus' coming. We should be prepared for it to happen any time at all. Jesus should find us working for him and honoring him whenever he returns.

Thank you, (*name*), you were a terrific helper. Let's all try to be alert so that we're ready to welcome Jesus at any time.   **—L.W.**

Second Sunday in Advent

———————————— • ————————————

The Gospel: Mark 1:1-8

Focus: John the Baptist was sent to prepare people for Jesus' coming.

Experience: Children will learn that John the Baptist had an important job to do.

Here Comes Jesus!

Do you like parades? Is there any special parade you like most? (*Let children respond.*) What do you like to see at a parade? (*Let the children respond.*) When I was about your age, I loved the Fourth of July parade. There were always lots of bands, old cars, fire engines, colorful floats, and bikes. We'd stand along the parade route and wait and wait and wait for the parade to come along. Finally, we'd hear music, very faint at first but getting louder. Then we'd know the parade was on its way at last!

John the Baptist lived at the time when Jesus was on the earth. He was a little like the music that tells you the parade is on its way. He had to tell everyone that someone special was coming. Do you know who that was? (*Let them answer.*) Yes, it was Jesus.

People had been expecting a Messiah for a long time—someone who would be their teacher and helper. God sent John to tell them all, "Here he comes! He will baptize you with the Holy Spirit while I can baptize you only with water. Get ready for him! He is so special that I am not worthy even to untie his sandals." John knew that Jesus was the Messiah.

John sounds a little odd, actually. The Bible says he wore clothes made of camel hair and he ate bugs! John kept telling people to repent—that is, to stop doing wrong things and to start doing things that are loving. This didn't make him very popular. However, John didn't mind if people thought he was strange. He knew what God wanted him to do. He was like the first, faint sounds of music before a parade. He was telling the world, "Get ready! Here comes the one you've been waiting for! The Messiah is coming at last!"

So when we hear about John the Baptist, let's remember he was the one who told us Jesus was coming.   **—L.W.**

Third Sunday in Advent
———————————— • ————————————

The Gospel: John 1:1-8, 19-28

Focus: The light shines in the darkness, and the darkness has not overcome it.

Experience: Children will see Christmas lights as a symbol of Jesus, the light of the world.

Christmas Lights

How many of you have your Christmas decorations up? (*They respond*.) Are there any decorations that you especially like? (*They answer*.)

You know what I like? I like the lights. All over town I see Christmas lights. Outside there are trees and bushes decorated with lights. Some people outline their entire house in lights. Inside, Christmas trees shine with strings of lights, and candles glow in the windows. Even though it gets dark early, the lights make everything beautiful.

The Bible tells us Jesus is the light of the world. John 1:5 says, "The light shines in the darkness, and the darkness did not overcome it." It's a good reminder that even though bad things sometimes happen, God is present and his light shines steadily.

When bad things happen, do you ever get scared? What are some things that make you feel scared? (*Allow for responses*.) Sometimes I feel afraid when the lights go out during a storm and the house is suddenly all dark. Then a flashlight is turned on or a candle is lighted, and we can see again. It's not so scary.

Close your eyes and cover them with your hands. (*Wait for children to do this*.) Is it dark in there? Now open your eyes. The light was here all the time even when you couldn't see it. That's how it is with God. God is always with us no matter what happens.

At Christmas the lights really brighten up the night. Even on the darkest nights the lights make everything look warm and cheerful. Let the lights this season remind you of God's love that is always with us. Remember that his son, Jesus, is the light of the world. The light shines in the darkness, and the darkness has not overcome it.
                                                                                        —L.W.

Fourth Sunday in Advent

———————————————•———————————————

The Gospel: Luke 1:26-38

Focus: Mary said yes to God even though she didn't know what to expect.

Experience: You will ask one of the children to do something that would be impossible to do alone. Since you want the child to succeed in this task, you help him or her. Similarly, when God has a job for us to do, he gives us strength to do it.

Preparation: Think up at least one task a child could do with your help but could not do alone. It could be to touch something that's too high for the child to reach or to lift something heavy. The example given below is the task of speaking a foreign language. Your dialogue will vary according to the task you select.

The Lord's Servant

I need someone with a good, strong voice to help me. (*Name of child*), will you be my helper? Oh, good. Now, it's almost Christmas, and I want to say "Merry Christmas" to as many people as possible. I'll say it in English and Hindi, and I want you to say it in Spanish. Be sure to speak loudly. Can you do that? (*The child may appear confused or say no.*) No? Why not? (*I don't know how.*) Oh, well, I'll tell you what. First I'll teach you how to say it. Then you can teach some of the others. In Spanish we say Merry Christmas like this: *Feliz Navidad.* (*Encourage the child to practice.*) That sounds great! Now, I'll go first. Then you can say what you have learned and teach it to the other children. (*Speak to the children.*) I wish you all Merry Christmas. *Subhechcha* (*shoo VECH chya*) Christmas— that's Hindi! Now, let's teach them how to say it in Spanish. (*Give the child a chance to speak. Say it along with him or her if help is needed.*)

Very good, (*name*)! I knew you could do it! All you needed was a little help.

Boys and girls, why did I help (*name*)? (*So the child could do what you asked.*) I wanted (*name*) to do this, so would it have made any sense for me to say, "Too bad you can't do it. I'm not going to help you. You'll just have to try it alone"? (*No. She or he couldn't have done the job alone.*)

When God's angel told Mary she would be the mother of Jesus, Mary didn't know what to expect. She had never been a mother before. She may have wondered what it would involve and how to explain it to Joseph and to her family. But Mary trusted God to help her. She said, "Here am I, the servant of the Lord." She knew that if God wanted her to be Jesus' mother, God would help her with everything she needed.

Someday you may have to do something that seems impossible or at least very difficult. You may not think you are able to do it, just as (*name*) did not think (*he or she*) could do what I asked. But remember, with a little help, (*name*) could do what I asked. And you can do hard things too because there is always someone there who can help you.

Who helps you? (*Children may say parents, friends, teachers, and so on. Affirm these responses and then encourage them to name God if they have not already done so.*) That's right! Just like Mary we should be ready and willing to be God's servants. God loves you and is always with you to help you and care for you.   **—L.W.**

The Nativity of Our Lord—Christmas Eve
—————————————————•—————————————————

The Gospel: Luke 2:1-20

Focus: Jesus' true identity was hidden by his human form.

Experience: The children will talk about Jesus as God's gift to us and learn that people did not recognize him as the Messiah.

Preparation: Bring two boxes: one plain and unwrapped, the other a beautifully wrapped present. Inside them, you could put toys for needy children, perhaps a more desirable toy in the plain box. Otherwise the plain box could contain treats for the children, and the other box could contain crumpled paper.

Christmas Secrets

Christmas is a great time for secrets, isn't it? We spend a lot of time making or buying presents for our family and friends. We sneak them into the house and hide them so no one will see them before Christmas. We try not to tell anybody what they're getting from us. We wrap the packages so that people won't know what their gifts are. All they can see is the wrapping until they open the box.

I have a secret right here. (*Show your wrapped box.*) Can you tell what's in here? (*Pass the box around for them to shake. Allow some guesses.*) Those would all be great gifts, but there's just no way to tell from the outside, is there? (*No.*)

I have another present too! (*Hold up the plain box. Then pass it around and allow them to shake and handle it.*) What do you think might be inside this present? (*Again, allow some guesses but don't focus on the contents.*) If you could choose only one present to open, which one would you choose? (*Probably the wrapped gift.*) Do you think one might have a nicer present inside? Maybe or maybe not. There's no way to tell from the outside, but which one looks more interesting to you? (*Probably the wrapped gift. Open both boxes and show what was inside, perhaps toys for needy children or crumpled paper in the wrapped box and treats in the plain box as suggested in the Preparation section.*)

God has given us many gifts: our homes, our families, our lives. But God has given us one very special gift. Who can tell me what that gift is? (*Affirm any other responses, but encourage them to name*

Jesus.) That's right! Jesus was God's very special gift to us. God had promised to send this gift to us for many, many years. God promised to send the Messiah—someone who would help the people and show them how to live. The people expected the Messiah to be someone like a great king—someone who was strong and mighty, rich and powerful. That's the way we are when we look for the biggest and most beautiful present to open first. We think that in order for something special to be inside, the outside should look special too.

But Jesus was more like this plain box. He was born in a stable not a palace. His parents were not rich and powerful. He was the son of a carpenter and a peasant girl. Though he looked like an ordinary baby, he had a great secret. He was God's Son—the Messiah the people had been waiting for.

A few people knew the secret. The angels told the shepherds who he was. The Wise Men knew. However, most people saw an ordinary baby. That's what he looked like.

As Jesus began his ministry, other people caught on too. He may have looked like an ordinary man, but he wasn't. Jesus is God's Son—our Messiah. And when he rose from his grave on Easter, still more people figured out the secret. On the outside he may have looked like everyone else, but he wasn't. He was the Christ, the Savior, the Messiah. He didn't come with power and riches. He wasn't like this fancy package. Those who came to know Jesus learned how special he was. They believed in him and became known as Christians.

We know the secret too. We know who Jesus is. I hope that when you open your Christmas gifts, every package will remind you of Jesus. Remember that God sent Jesus to be our Messiah. Tonight we say thank you to God for this wonderful gift.   **—L.W.**

The Nativity of Our Lord—Christmas Day

The Gospel: John 1:1-14

Focus: Christmas is Jesus' birthday. We should give him a present.

Experience: The children will think about what they can do for Jesus.

Preparation: Bring a bag or basket of small gifts (candy canes or even colorful bows), one for each child in the group. You will use these as "birthday gifts" for each child.

Happy Birthday, Jesus

(*If you have a very small group, you may wish to ask each child the following two questions. If there are more than six or seven, ask only a couple of the children. . . .*) When is your birthday? (*Allow the child to answer.*) Do you usually have a birthday party? (*Response.*) Do the rest of you have parties? (*Yes.*) What do you do when you have a birthday party? (*If no one mentions getting presents, prompt them with the question, "Do your guests bring anything?" Pick one child to be your "birthday child."*)

We're going to pretend to have a birthday party right now. First, I need some help. (*Choose someone.*) (*Name child*), let's pretend it's your birthday today. Come stand beside me here. (*Give the child the bag or basket, and tell her or him to distribute one gift to each child. When everyone has received one, continue talking.*)

Wow, this is odd. We said it was (*Name child*)'s birthday party, but who has the gifts? The rest of you do! That's backwards, isn't it? And yet that's what happens at Christmas. Whose birthday is it? (*Jesus'.*) Right! But *we* get all the presents! Jesus doesn't get anything. (*Give the child a gift and let her or him sit down.*)

The Bible says the Wise Men brought gifts to Jesus: gold, frankincense, and myrrh. Some songs say that a little drummer boy played for him and the animals shared their stable with him. Maybe we could give Jesus something for his birthday. When we give gifts, we try to give things that will make the other person happy. What do you think would make Jesus happy? (*If children are on the wrong track or have no ideas, you may need to ask things like, "Do you think it makes him happy if you help someone? How about when you fight with your brothers and sisters? Is he happy when you obey your parents?" Other possibilities are: reading the Bible, being unselfish, caring for an animal, helping a sibling or refusing to do wrong, and showing love for others.)*

We receive so much at Christmas! We get so many gifts! Jesus himself is a gift—from God to us. Today, for Christmas, let's each find some way to give a present to Jesus. After all, it is his birthday! *(You could close by singing together "Happy Birthday to Jesus.")*—**L.W.**

First Sunday after Christmas

————————————— • —————————————

The Gospel: Luke 2:25-40

Focus: The Holy Spirit revealed Jesus' identity to Simeon.

Experience: Children will learn that the Holy Spirit helps us to know Jesus.

Preparation: Bring a picture of Jesus that shows a halo around his head. Also bring at least one other picture of someone in similar clothing—maybe a disciple.

Simeon Knew

You're going to be detectives today. I brought a couple of pictures with me. I want you to see if you can tell me which picture shows Jesus. (*Show pictures.*)

What do you think? Which picture is of Jesus? (*They answer.*) How did you know that was the right one? (*Because of the halo.*) Yes, we often see pictures of Jesus with a halo. But, you know, I don't think Jesus really had a halo. There were a lot of people who had no idea that Jesus was anybody special. If he had had a halo, don't you think people would have noticed it? Then they'd ask what it was, and Jesus would have to explain that it showed he was the Son of God. The Bible doesn't tell us anything like that. I think the person who painted this picture wanted to do something to show that Jesus is special.

One man who recognized Jesus as the Messiah was named Simeon. When Joseph and Mary took the baby Jesus to the temple, Simeon knew immediately who he was even without a halo. He picked Jesus up and thanked God that he had been allowed to see Jesus with his own eyes.

How did Simeon know who Jesus was? The Bible tells us that the Holy Spirit told Simeon. Simeon could have said, "Are you sure? That looks like any other baby to me. Let me watch him for a while. If I decide you're right, then I'll go speak to him and his parents." But that's not what Simeon did. He knew who Jesus was. He had been waiting for a long, long time. Simeon went up to Jesus at once.

It is the Holy Spirit's job to help us know Jesus. God doesn't usually blow trumpets or shout or put halos on people to get our attention. We have to learn to listen for the Spirit during church, in Sunday school, in our prayers, and in other places. The Holy Spirit helps us know Jesus just as the Spirit helped Simeon. We have to be ready to listen when the Spirit talks to us.   **—L.W.**

Second Sunday after Christmas

———————————————— • ————————————————

The Gospel: John 1:1-18

Focus: God is eternal.

Experience: You and the children will contrast the imperma-
nence of everyday things, symbolized by soap bubbles, with the
eternal constancy of God.

Preparation: Bring a bottle of commercial soap bubble mixture.

In the Beginning Was God

(*Blow some soap bubbles before you begin to speak and after each of the
opening sentences, up to the instruction to sigh. Quite likely the children
will try to chase and break the bubbles.*) Pretty, aren't they? What
lovely colors! They're fun to blow too. There's just one problem.
They're very fragile. They don't last. (*Sigh.*) Do any of you think
you could blow a bubble so big that it would last all the way
through my talk? (*Let volunteers try.*) No, they don't last, no matter
how careful we are or how hard we try to make them last. They're
here, and then they're gone.

Most things in life are that way. A lot of the things you got last
Christmas are broken or lost or you've gotten tired of them, right?
Maybe that's true of some of the things you got *this* Christmas! You
outgrow your favorite clothes, or they become too stained or torn
to wear. You get a teacher you love, but you have to leave her or
him for another class when school ends. Friends move away.
Books and games you used to love become too easy for you. Things
don't last forever. They're like (*blow soap bubbles*) these bubbles.

There's only one thing that lasts forever and doesn't change. Do
you know what that is? (*Let them guess. If they guess "God," agree and
go on. If nobody guesses, say, "Let me give you some hints."*) The Bible
says, "In the beginning was the Word, and the Word was with
God, and the Word was God" (John 1:1). The Bible says, "For I the
Lord do not change" (Malachi 3:6). The Bible says, "I have loved
you with an everlasting love" (Jeremiah 31:3). The Bible says, "The
faithfulness of the Lord endures forever" (Psalm 117:2).

God has existed since the very beginning and he goes on forever. He loved us before we were born, loves us now, and will love

us throughout eternity. There is no one and nothing else that is eternal. There is no one else whose love is so unchanging—only God. Day in, day out, year after year, his everlasting arms support us.

We love Christmas, but it doesn't last forever. Your Christmas decorations will be taken down soon if they aren't down already. But remember, the one whose birth we celebrate at Christmas *does* last. Jesus was in the beginning, is now, and ever shall be. In the beginning—in the very beginning—was God.   **—L.W.**

The Epiphany of Our Lord

———————————————•———————————————

The Gospel: Matthew 2:1-12

Focus: Jesus is our Savior and our King.

Experience: The children will become familiar with the story of the Wise Men by helping to retell the story.

The Wise Men

Today is the day we call *Epiphany*. That's kind of a funny word, isn't it? Epiphany. Can you say it? (*Response.*)

The word *Epiphany* means "to show." It's the name of this church season; and during the next few weeks, the Bible stories you hear in church will *show* you who Jesus is. On Christmas we talked about Jesus being born. Now during Epiphany, we will look at who this Jesus is.

We start Epiphany by looking at a very special story. I'm sure it's one that many of you have heard. It's the story of the Wise Men coming to see Jesus when he was small.

The story begins by telling us that there were Wise Men who lived far away in the east. They wanted to find Jesus. Do you remember the name of the town where Jesus was born? (*Bethlehem.*)

Yes. Jesus was born in a small town called Bethlehem. And the Wise Men lived far to the east of that. We aren't exactly sure where the Wise Men lived, but we think it was a long way from Bethlehem.

The Wise Men learned that a new king was born. They found out because of something they saw in the sky. Who can remember what they saw? (*A star.*)

That's right! The Wise Men saw a bright, bright star in the sky. They believed that the bright new star announced the birth of a king. So they followed the star to the country of Judea, where Jesus was.

When the Wise Men arrived in Judea, they went to the capital city, the city of Jerusalem. I suppose they figured that a new king would be born in the palace. So they went to the palace, and they met the man who was the king. Do you know what the king's name was? (*Herod.*) King Herod, yes. Now Herod was a mean king. He wasn't very nice. The Wise Men came to Herod and said they wanted to worship the newborn king. Well, Herod was very jealous. *He* was the king! He didn't want any newborn king in his land, so he started thinking about how he could kill Jesus. He asked some priests where the new king was to be born. The priests told him Bethlehem. So Herod told the Wise Men to go to Bethlehem and find the newborn king and then come back and tell Herod where the king was. Herod told the Wise Men a lie. He told them he too wanted to go and worship Jesus. But Herod really wanted to know where Jesus was so he could kill him.

The Wise Men left and went to Bethlehem. Bethlehem is only five miles from Jerusalem. (*You may want to name a nearby town or area to compare the mileage.*) The Bible says the Wise Men followed the star right to the place where Jesus was.

Jesus was still very young, so he was with his parents. What were the names of Jesus' parents? (*Mary and Joseph.*) That's right! The Wise Men went in, and what did they do? (*They worshiped Jesus and gave him gifts.*) Yes. The Wise Men gave Jesus gifts of gold and myrrh and frankincense. Those are very expensive items—gifts fit for a king! The Wise Men gave Jesus gifts and worshiped him.

When they decided it was time to leave, did they go back to King Herod? (*No.*) No, they didn't. The Bible says that God told the Wise Men in a dream not to go to Herod because Herod wanted to hurt Jesus. So the Wise Men went back home a different way. And Herod didn't find out where Jesus was.

This really is a great story, isn't it? It reminds us how good it is to worship Jesus. But even more, this story shows us that Jesus is King. On this day that we call Epiphany let's remember that Jesus has come to be our Savior and our King.   **—M.B.**

The Baptism of Our Lord—First Sunday in Epiphany

The Gospel: Mark 1:4-11

Focus: In the baptism of Jesus God declares that Jesus is his Son, the Beloved. In our Baptism God declares that we too are his children, loved by him.

Experience: Talk with the children about the story of Jesus' baptism. Then point out that in our Baptism, God declares us to be his children.

Baptized!

Today's Gospel reading tells about Jesus' baptism. Do you remember the story? I thought we'd talk today about Jesus' baptism.

Think for a moment: where was Jesus baptized? Was he baptized in a church? (*No, the Jordan River.*)

That's right. Jesus was baptized in a river: the Jordan River. Do you remember who baptized Jesus? (*John the Baptist.*) Yes. John the Baptist lived out in the wilderness by the Jordan River. John was a preacher who told people about God and baptized them in the river.

We think that Jesus was about thirty years old when he went to John and asked to be baptized. John and Jesus probably walked out into the Jordan River together and John baptized Jesus there in the river.

Now as Jesus was coming out of the water, a voice from heaven spoke—a very special voice. Who do you think it was? (*God.*)

Yes. God said, "You are my Son, the Beloved; with you I am well pleased." God was saying, "Jesus is my Son, and I love him very much."

And do you know what? When you were baptized, God spoke too! Oh he didn't speak from heaven like at Jesus' baptism. God used the pastor to speak for him. But when you were baptized, the pastor spoke God's Word. And what the pastor said was that you are now a child of God. The pastor said, (*speak the names of as many children as you can*) "You are now children of God, and God loves you very, very much."

That's the great thing about baptism. When we were baptized,

God made us his children. And God promised to love us each and every day of our lives.

So today let's remember baptism. Jesus was baptized, and God said, "This is my beloved Son." We too have been baptized. And God said we are his children, and he loves us very much. **—M.B.**

Second Sunday in Epiphany

─────────────────────●─────────────────────

The Gospel: John 1:43-51

Focus: Jesus makes us special. As we follow him, we become presents given for others.

Experience: Tying a ribbon around the wrist of each child will help remind them that in Jesus they are special presents given to other people.

Preparation: Bring a nicely wrapped present with a ribbon around it. Also bring extra ribbons cut in eight-inch lengths to tie on the wrist of each of the children. An option is to use commercial bows with the sticky surface uncovered. You might have some adults or older children available to help tie or put on the ribbons.

Ribbons and Presents

I brought a present with me today. (*Show the children the present.*) Do you like to receive presents? I know I do.

Notice the ribbon on this present. Sometimes we put ribbons on presents. When we give someone a present, we say, "Here is something for you."

I'd like to put a ribbon on each of you today because I think each one of you is special. You are special because Jesus loves you very much. In the love of Jesus we are all very special and important.

In fact, each one of you is a present. Did you know that? Do you think you could be a present for someone? (*Allow for responses.*) How could you be a present? (*Helping, caring, sharing, and so on.*) You see, Jesus teaches us to love and care for other people. As we do that, as we help and care for other people, we become presents given to them. We become very special presents who love and care for others.

So, I'd like to put ribbons on you. I thought I'd tie one on your wrist (or place a bow on your shirt or dress). Would you like to have a ribbon? Great! (*Put a ribbon on a wrist of each of the children or a bow on their clothes. This will take a few minutes. If necessary, have some adults or older children help you.*)

There, we all have ribbons. We have ribbons because we are special presents. When you see your ribbon, first remember that Jesus makes you special. And then remember that you are a present given by God to others. As we share with people and help people, we are very special presents.   **—M.B.**

Third Sunday in Epiphany
————————————•————————————

The Gospel: Mark 1:14-20

Focus: Jesus calls his followers to "fish for people."

Experience: Talk with the children and act out how to fish. Then talk about Jesus' call to "fish for people."

Preparation: If possible, bring a fishing pole and bobber (no hooks!). If not, pretend along with the children.

Going Fishing

I thought we'd talk today about going fishing. Have any of you ever gone fishing? Have you ever caught any fish? (*Give the children a chance to answer.*)

What do you use to go fishing? (*Allow responses and affirm them.*) You need a fishing pole. (If you have a pole, show them.) Of course you have a line coming from the pole. On the end of the line you put a hook with some bait on it. And you put a bobber on the string. Then you cast the bait out into the water.

Let's pretend we are fishing. Do you all have your fishing poles? (*Have the children pretend they are holding fishing poles.*) Let's cast our bait out into the water. (*Pretend to cast.*) Come on, cast out your bait.

OK, our bait is in the water. And the bobber goes down. What does that mean? (*You have a fish.*) We have a fish. So what do we do? (*Pull it in. Pretend to reel in a fish. Have the children act it out with you.*) There, we've caught our fish. That's how we fish nowadays.

In today's Gospel reading two men named Simon and Andrew were fishing. Only they fished a little differently back in those days. Back then, fishermen used big nets. What they did was, they threw the nets out into the water. (*Pretend you are throwing a net.*) The fish would get caught in the net. Then they would pull in the net with all the fish. (*Pretend to pull in a net.*)

Let's try fishing that way. Throw out your nets. (*Have the children pretend to throw out nets.*) Do you think you have any fish? Let's pull them in. (*Pretend to pull in the nets.*) Did you catch any? (*Allow responses.*) Did you catch a lot of fish? (*Allow responses.*) Good for you.

In our Gospel reading Simon and Andrew were fishing. They were casting out their nets. Jesus came along and said, "Follow me and I will make you fish for people." That's an interesting thing for Jesus to say. What does Jesus mean, fish for people? (*Give the children a chance to respond. If they can't, be prepared to continue.*)

Jesus wanted Simon and Andrew to become disciples. Disciples are people who help catch people for God. To fish for people means that you tell people about God and invite them to believe in Jesus. You don't use poles or nets. You tell people about God. And that is what Simon and Andrew did. They became disciples who told people about God.

Jesus wants us to help fish for people too. He wants us to help catch people for God. Can you think of some ways that we can fish for people? (*Give the children a chance to answer. Be prepared to help them with suggestions such as, "We can tell people about Jesus" or "We can invite people to church" or "We can help people and care for them."*) Yes. Those are good ways that we can fish for people.

Remember, it is fun to go fishing. It's fun to fish for fish. And it is even more special to tell people about God. When we follow Jesus, we fish for people.   **—M.B.**

Fourth Sunday in Epiphany
———————————————•———————————————

The Gospel: Mark 1:21-28

Focus: The Gospel focuses on Jesus' authority and power over evil. This sermon will remind the children of Jesus' ability to take care of them and will direct the children to Jesus.

Experience: Children often feel afraid, especially at night. Nightmares and "night terrors" are quite common. In this sermon children will discover that Jesus cares for them, especially when they are afraid at night.

Jesus Takes Care of Us

Sometimes I feel a little bit afraid. How about you? Do you ever get scared (*Probably yes.*) I think we all do. I think there are times when all of us are scared or afraid.

Sometimes I get scared at night. Do you ever get scared at night? (*Yes.*) Nighttimes can be scary. Sometimes when it's dark and I'm alone, I hear a noise and I get worried. Or sometimes I have a bad dream and I wake up and I'm scared. I remember once when I was little, I watched a monster movie late one night. I think I was scared of the dark for the next month!

What scares you, or worries you? (*Let the children talk about things that scare them. Talk about nightmares or strange noises or fears of monsters. Be affirming and supportive.*)

Yes, those are all things that can scare us. We all have times of being afraid.

But I've learned something. I've learned that Jesus takes care of us. I've learned that especially when we are scared, and especially when we are alone at night, Jesus takes care of us.

In today's Gospel reading there is a man who has some big problems, and he probably felt afraid too. But Jesus is strong. Jesus took care of the man. And Jesus is strong enough to take care of us too.

Do you know what I do when I'm afraid at night? You can do this too. When I'm afraid, I talk to Jesus. I say, "Jesus, come and protect me. Thank you, Jesus." Can you say that with me? (*Repeat it together a few times.*)

That's a good thing to say at night. And do you know what?

Jesus does just that. He comes and he protects us. That's why I say "thank you." Jesus does come and take care of us.

So remember, Jesus will take care of you. If you are scared some night or you wake up after a bad dream or you are just worried about something, talk to Jesus. Say, "Jesus, come and protect me." Jesus is stronger than anything that can hurt us and he will take care of us.

Let's pray together the prayer I just taught you: "Jesus, come and protect us. Thank you, Jesus. Amen."   —M.B.

Fifth Sunday in Epiphany

———————————————•———————————————

The Gospel: Mark 1:29-39

Focus: Jesus' ministry is directed to all people. We too should welcome all.

Experience: The children will talk about the church being a place that welcomes all.

Preparation: Have a doormat that says "Welcome" on it. (If you have such a mat in front of one of your church doors, use that one!)

Welcome!

I brought a doormat with me today. (*Hold up the doormat.*) Have you ever seen a doormat? What are doormats for? (*Wiping your feet.*)

That's right. Often our feet get dirty or muddy. So we wipe them on doormats before we go into a building. I remember when I was a youngster, my mother would always tell me, "Wipe your feet before you come into the house." I guess she didn't want me to bring in a lot of dirt to get on the floor.

This doormat has a word on it. What does it say? (*Welcome.*) Yes, welcome. What does the word *welcome* mean? (*It means that you can come in; you are wanted here.*) Yes, welcome means to come on in; we're glad you're here! Welcome. Come in and join us!

Let me ask you a question. Who is welcome here in our church? Who is welcome here? (*Give the children a chance to think and answer. Affirm a variety of answers: our members, the pastor, everybody.*)

That's right. Everybody is welcome here: young, old, rich, poor, black, white, Hispanic, Oriental, members, nonmembers—*everybody* is welcome here. Jesus wants everyone to come to his church. He is concerned for everybody.

That's part of what is so much fun about being a church. We welcome everybody to come here and share in God's family. Our church is for everybody.

What can we do to show that everybody is welcome here? (*Affirm a variety of responses: say hello, introduce ourselves, give directions, sit near visitors, and others.*) Today, I want each of you to think of some way you can welcome people into our congregation. Let's tell everyone, ''We're glad you're here! Welcome!''

(*If appropriate, you could leave the doormat outside the front door.*)

—M.B.

Sixth Sunday in Epiphany
————————————————— • —————————————————

The Gospel: Mark 1:40-45

Focus: The Gospel tells about Jesus helping an outcast. Jesus shows us that all people have value.

Experience: You will show the children an old dollar bill and ask them to throw it away. Point out that people, even more than dollar bills, always have worth.

Preparation: Bring an old crinkled, worn dollar bill.

Always Special

I brought a dollar bill with me today. (*Show the dollar bill to the children.*) It's an old dollar bill. It's faded and wrinkled. It looks like it's almost worn out. As old as this dollar bill is, I should probably just throw it away. What do you think? (*No!*) No? Why not? It's wrinkled. It's faded. It looks terrible. Why shouldn't we just get rid of it? (*It's worth a dollar. You can buy things with it.*) So you never throw dollar bills away? (*No, never.*) Of course, you are right. A dollar bill is always special, isn't it? It's always worth something. No matter what it looks like, you can always buy things with it. A dollar bill is always special.

I think people are like a dollar bill. People are always special too. No matter what we look like, no matter what happens to us, people are always special. Each person is a unique gift of God. Each person is important.

In today's Gospel reading, there is a man who has a disease called leprosy. In Bible times, people who had leprosy could not live with their families. They had to go away from others. They were outcasts. Do you know what an outcast is? (*Someone people don't like; someone people are afraid of.*) That's right. An outcast is someone that people don't like or want to be with. The man in the story was an outcast. But Jesus saw him, cared for him, and healed him. Jesus knew the man was special.

Jesus teaches us that all people are special. Like this dollar bill (*hold up the dollar bill again*) we may get crinkled and wrinkled, but we're always special—each of us is important. You and I and everybody we meet are gifts of God. In Jesus all people are important.   **—M.B.**

Seventh Sunday in Epiphany
——————————————•——————————————

The Gospel: Mark 2:1-12

Focus: Jesus is God's Son, who loves us, forgives us, and helps us.

Experience: The children will use their imaginations in order to appreciate the story of Jesus and the man who was paralyzed.

There's a Hole in the Roof!

Today's Gospel is about Jesus healing a man who couldn't move. Jesus was in a house. A large crowd of people came to the house, and they all wanted to see Jesus. There were so many people that they were packed in. They were squeezed in on top of each other.

Let's pretend that we are in that house. To do that, let's all squeeze in real tight together, so we feel like we're packed into the house. Everybody squeeze in. (*Have the children move close together.*)

Great! We're all in the house. We're crowded, and we're all listening to Jesus. Jesus is over there (*indicate somewhere a short distance from you.*)

Well, four people came to the house, carrying a friend of theirs. The friend was lying on a mat—a large board, only softer. Their friend was paralyzed. Do you know what it means to be paralyzed? (*You can't move.*) That's right. Their friend was paralyzed. He couldn't move. He couldn't walk. He just lay there on the mat. The four people brought this man to Jesus, hoping that Jesus would heal him.

Let's pretend this is the doorway. When the men came, to the house, what did they find? (*It was too crowded to get through.*) With all of us here they couldn't get to Jesus.

So what did the friends do? Do you remember the Bible story I just read? (*Give the children a chance to answer. If they can't, simply continue.*) The friends climbed up on the roof. They started digging a hole in the roof. Now in our day if you wanted a hole in a roof, you would need a saw, and you have to cut a hole. But back in Jesus' time, roofs were made out of branches and dirt and clay with thin boards or tiles underneath. The man's friends could dig through that and lift up a board or two.

When the hole was big enough, they very carefully let their friend down through the hole. So there was this man on a mat being let down from the roof. (*Motion with your hands to reinforce the story.*)

Now as you watch all this, what are you thinking? How do you feel as you see this man coming down from a hole in the roof? (*Be prepared to prompt the children. "Are you surprised, worried?" Affirm their reponses.*)

It would be pretty surprising, wouldn't it? Here came this man. He was let down right in front of Jesus. And what did Jesus do? He looked at the man and said two things. First, he said, "Your sins are forgiven." Then Jesus said a second thing. What else did Jesus say? (*Get up and walk.*)

That's right. Rise and walk. And the man did! This man couldn't move before. But now he got up and he could walk. He was healed! How do you think the man felt? (*Very happy, surprised, thankful.*) What did the people think? (*The people were amazed. They wondered, Who is this Jesus?*)

Well, we know Jesus. He is God's Son. He came to forgive sins. And he came to take care of people. In fact, that is who Jesus still is today. He is God's Son, who forgives us and takes care of us.

That's the story in today's Gospel. It's a great story: some men bring their friend to Jesus, and Jesus helps him. The story reminds us who Jesus is. Jesus is God's Son, who forgives us and takes care of us. **—M.B.**

Eighth Sunday in Epiphany
——————————————— • ———————————————

The Gospel: Mark 2:18-22

Focus: The Gospel announces that God is doing a new thing through Jesus Christ. Our response to that is to praise God.

Experience: The children will talk about cheering at sports events and compare cheering to praising and worshiping God.

Preparation: Think of a phrase from the worship service that the children can use as a cheer. Phrases such as *Thanks be to God*, *Alleluia*, or *Praise the Lord* work well.

Praise God!

How many of you have ever gone to a football game or basketball game? What do you do there? (*Watch, eat, talk, cheer. Affirm their responses.*) Do you ever cheer for your favorite team? (*Responses*). It's fun to cheer. Tell me, how do you cheer? What are some things you do? (*Yell, stomp our feet, clap.*) Yes, those are all things we do to cheer: we yell, "De-fense," we stomp our feet, we whistle, we clap. It's fun to be in a crowd that is cheering. Why do we cheer? (*Because we like our team, we're excited, we like to be involved.*) Yes, we cheer to say that we're proud of our team. We support them. This is our team.

I've been thinking about our worship service lately. I think there are some times in worship when we cheer. We cheer for God. We may not yell or stomp our feet, but there are some special things we do in worship. And what we are really doing is cheering for God. We say, "This is our God. We're glad for all God does. We love God. We're excited about all God is doing."

Can you think of some ways we cheer for God in worship? (*Allow time for responses: sing, pray, thank God. If no responses are given, continue.*) One thing we do is sing. We sing things like, "Praise God from whom all blessings flow." To praise God is to say, "This is our God." And so when we sing, "Praise God," we are cheering for God.

Another way we cheer for God is to say things like "Thanks be to God," or "Alleluia." Those are all ways of cheering for God.

Let's work together to do a cheer for God. (*If your congregation uses these words at the close of worship, point this out to the children.*) I will say "Go in peace. Serve the Lord." And you all say, "Thanks be to God." That's a cheer. We're saying, "Thank you, God, for the great things you have done."

Let's cheer for God. I'll say, "Go in peace. Serve the Lord." And you say, "Thanks be to God." Are you ready? Go in peace. Serve the Lord. (*Thanks be to God!*)

Not bad. But it needs a little more life. Cheers should be loud and exciting. Let's try it again. Go in peace. Serve the Lord. (*Thanks be to God!*) That's great! We say, "Yes God, thank you for all that you do."

Remember, it's fun to cheer. When you go to a football game or a basketball game, be sure to cheer for your team. And in worship we cheer for God. It's important to thank and praise our God.

Let's close with one more cheer. Are you ready? Go in peace. Serve the Lord. (*Thanks be to God!*)   **—M.B.**

The Transfiguration of Our Lord— Last Sunday in Epiphany

—————————————— • ——————————————

The Gospel: Mark 9:2-9

Focus: The transfiguration proclaims the lordship of Jesus.

Experience: The children will learn how to say "Jesus Christ is Lord" in Spanish. If another language is prominent in your area (Vietnamese, German, Laotian), teach the children to say "Jesus Christ is Lord" in that language.

Preparation: Learn how to say "Jesus Christ is Lord" in Spanish or in some other language. "Jesus Christ is Lord" in Spanish is *Jesucristo es Señor* (HAY-soo CREES-toh ehs sane-YOUR).

Jesucristo es Señor

I'd like to teach you a sentence in another language today. Do any of you know Spanish? (*Allow time for responses.*) I'd like to teach you a sentence in Spanish.

The sentence is this: Jesucristo es Señor. Let's try that. Try to repeat it after me. (*Say one word at a time, slowly, and allow time for them to repeat after you. Then say the entire phrase and have them repeat it.*)

Very good. You just said a sentence in Spanish. It's fun and good to learn another language. Do you know what you said? You said, "Jesus Christ is Lord." "Jesucristo es Señor" means "Jesus Christ is Lord." Can you say it with me one more time? (*Jesucristo es Señor.*)

Jesus Christ is Lord. That's something we say in church quite a bit. Let me ask you a question. What does it mean to say that Jesus is Lord? (*Give the children a chance to answer. If they can't, simply continue.*) To say that Jesus is Lord means that he is our king. He is the most important person for us to know. In fact, he is the Son of God, who loves us and who saves us. He is the most important person for you and me.

Jesus Christ is Lord. Whether we say that in English or Spanish or Vietnamese or German, there is nothing more important to say. You see, Jesus is Lord over the whole world. And he wants all people to believe in him.

Let's say our sentence one more time and let's have the rest of the congregation join us. (*Have the children say the sentence with you.*) Very good! Now you know a sentence in Spanish. And remember, Jesus Christ is Lord!   **—M.B.**

First Sunday in Lent
—————————————•—————————————

The Gospel: Mark 1:12-15

Focus: Jesus resisted the devil's temptations in the wilderness. We can be like him when temptation comes our way.

Experience: The children will hear about how Jesus said no to temptation, and they will talk about saying no themselves.

How to Say No

Today's Bible story says that Jesus was tempted by the devil. Do you know what it means to be tempted? (*Allow responses.*) Being tempted means that you think about doing something that you know is wrong.

The Bible tells us that Jesus was in the wilderness for forty days. That's a long time. It's more than a month! All during that time, Jesus was alone, and he didn't have anything to eat. By the end of that time, how do you think Jesus was feeling? (*Tired, hungry, lonely.*) Yes, he probably was tired and hungry, but when the devil tried to tempt him, what did Jesus always say? (*No.*) That's right. He always said "no." He told the devil that those things were wrong and that he was not going to do them.

Do you know what? The devil is still trying to tempt people. He gave up on tempting Jesus, but he hasn't given up trying to tempt the rest of us.

Do you ever think about doing something that you know you shouldn't do such as taking something that doesn't belong to you? (*Allow responses.*) Sometimes I do too, and the devil is happy when we feel that way. He is even happier when we go ahead and *do* the things we shouldn't.

But did you know that there is someone who will always help us do what is right? Do you know who can help us? (*God, Jesus, the Holy Spirit.*) Yes. We ask for help when we say the Lord's Prayer. "Lead us not into temptation, but deliver us from evil."

The next time you feel tempted to do something wrong, just stop and think, "What would Jesus say? What would Jesus do?" Thinking about Jesus makes it a lot easier to turn away from temptation. He turned away from it, and he'll help you turn away too.

—S.L.

Second Sunday in Lent

———————————•———————————

The Gospel: Mark 8:31-38

Focus: God is in charge of our lives. He knows what is best for us, and we should try to do God's will.

Experience: The children will discuss situations in which they and their parents might not agree as to what is best. The children will be encouraged to trust and follow their parents and God.

Who Is in Charge?

How many of you ever wanted to go outside without a coat, but your parents made you wear one? (*Allow responses.*) Why did they do that? (*They were concerned about you and didn't want you to get cold; they had listened to the weather report, they knew it was going to be a chilly day.*)

Did you ever ask to have a snack, and your parents told you to wait until after dinner? (*Allow responses.*) Why did they do that? (*You might get filled up and not be able to eat any dinner.*) Why do your parents want you to eat chicken and peas instead of cookies? (*You need food like chicken and peas in order to grow up strong and healthy. They care enough about you to insist that you eat properly even though you may not like it.*) In most situations parents and other grown-ups know more than children. They usually know what's best. They usually make the plans.

Do you ever get a little angry when you want something and your parents want something else for you? (*Allow responses.*)

In today's Bible story that's what happened to Peter. Jesus was explaining the plans that God had made for him. Peter didn't like the plans, and he told Jesus that they weren't very good plans. Jesus had to remind Peter that God's plan is always best.

God also has plans for you and for me. How can we find out God's plans for us? (*Allow responses.*) (*Sometimes our parents can tell us, from the Bible, at Sunday school and church, and by just talking with God.*) What is it called when you talk with God? (*Prayer.*) That's right. It's called praying. Children and grown-ups all need to talk to God in prayer. When we pray, we can ask for God's help to do what is right. Let's do that right now.

Dear God, thank you for listening to us when we pray. Thank you for being with us, for loving us, and for helping us to do the things you want us to do. Help us to always listen to you. Amen.

—S.L.

Third Sunday in Lent
————————————————•————————————————

The Gospel: John 2:13-22

Focus: We need to remember that the church is God's house and worshiping God is the most important purpose for coming to church.

Experience: The children will first discuss the purpose of school and then imagine what would happen if other activities crowded out learning at school. They will then do the same thing for their time in the church building.

Why Are We Here?

Do any of you go to school? (*Yes.*) What do you do there? (*Allow for responses.*) That's right! Many things happen at school, but the most important thing is *learning*. That's why the teachers are there—to help you learn.

What do you suppose would happen if they changed the schools? Right now, those of you who go to school probably have classes all morning, have a quick lunch, attend more classes, maybe have some free time or recess, and then you have more classes. Suppose they changed that. Suppose that the school day would start with an hour of free time, then a short time for classes, then an hour of recess, then lunch, then maybe one class, and then *two* hours of free time. This would be quite a change! What do you think would happen? (*Allow responses.*) You are right. It might be a lot of fun, but there wouldn't be much learning going on. Since the reason you go to school is to learn, this wouldn't be a good way to run a school.

In the Bible story today something like this happened in the Temple. A temple is a place of worship, like our church. People used a temple for many things, just as people use our church for many things. But really, temples and churches don't belong to *people*. Who do they belong to? (*God.*) Yes. Our church is really God's church, and the Temple in the Bible was God's too. Can you remember what happened in the Temple in today's reading? (*Jesus chased out those who were selling things. He was angry that people treated the Temple like the marketplace.*)

Sometimes we can get very busy here at church, too. We go to choir practice, work on Sunday school projects, put on programs, and bring food for hungry people. Some churches have scout troops, exercise classes, and all kinds of activities. These are all good things but sometimes we get so busy with them that we forget we are in church, and whose house is this? (*God's.*) That's right. Those other activities are OK, but the most important thing for us to do here is to worship and thank God, just as we are doing this morning in this church service.   **—S.L.**

Fourth Sunday in Lent

———————————•———————————

The Gospel: John 3:14-21

Focus: God loves each of us.

Experience: The children will learn to say "Jesus loves me," using sign language.

Preparation: Practice the following words in sign language so that you can comfortably teach them.

Jesus   **loves**   **me.**

Jesus Loves Me

Today's Gospel lesson has one of the best-known Bible verses in it. John 3:16 says: "For God so loved the world that he gave his only Son, so that everyone who believes in him may not perish but may have everlasting life." This verse tells us something very important about our life with God. It tells us how God feels about the world — how God feels about us. How does God feel about us? (*God loves us.*) That's right! God loves us — each one of us.

This verse also tells us something that God did because of that love. What did God do? (*He sent us Jesus.*) That's right! God sent his Son Jesus. He was born on earth as a little baby, and he grew up, just like you are growing up now.

When Jesus was older, he loved people and tried to teach them about God. What are some ways Jesus taught people about God? (*He told stories, healed sick people, taught his followers.*) That's right.

Jesus also was arrested, he suffered, and he died on the cross. Why do you think Jesus did all these things? (*Because he loves us.*) Yes. God loves you, and Jesus loves you. If you can't remember anything else about Jesus, remember that Jesus loves you.

I'd like to teach you a way to remember that Jesus loves you, using sign language. People who cannot hear or speak use sign language to communicate with each other. We can learn sign language too.

This is the sign for "Jesus." (*Demonstrate the sign.*) Now you try it. (*Allow some time for them to try the sign. Affirm their efforts and repeat the word together a few times.*)

This is the sign for "loves." (*Demonstrate the sign and repeat the previous process.*)

This is the sign for "me." You probably know it already! (*Demonstrate the sign and repeat the previous process.*)

Now, let's do all the signs so we can give the message, "Jesus loves me." (*Lead them in the three signs.*) That's wonderful! Now I want us to sing a song together and use these signs we have just learned. Let's sing together, "Jesus Loves Me." Get ready to use sign language! (*Lead them in the song, using sign language each time you say the words "Jesus loves me."*)

> Jesus loves me! this I know,
> For the Bible tells me so;
> Little ones to Him belong,
> They are weak but He is strong.
> Yes, Jesus loves me! (repeat two times)
> The Bible tells me so.
> —Anna B. Warner

That was really great! I hope that you will remember the sign language you learned today. Teach it to someone else, and help them to learn that Jesus loves them too!

Let's all bow our heads for a thank you prayer to God. Dear God, Thank you so much for sending Jesus for us. Please help us to remember how much you love us, and help us to share your love with others. Amen.   **—L.R.**

Fifth Sunday in Lent

———————————————•———————————————

The Gospel: John 12:20-33

Focus: Jesus' death makes possible our eternal life with God.

Experience: The children will see the promise of new life out of death by looking at a new bean sprout.

Preparation: One week before you deliver this sermon, plant a bean seed in a cup of dirt. Cover with about 3/4 inch of soil. Keep the soil moist and in a sunny spot. A plant should sprout in four or five days. Bring this seedling along with another cup of dirt, a bean seed, and a little cup of water. You might put the seedling and other materials in a paper bag or box to keep them out of sight until you need them.

As an additional treat, you might consider distributing seed packets to the children so that they can plant something at home and watch it grow. Marigolds are hardy plants that will grow either indoors or outdoors.

Life out of Death

Have any of you ever had company come to visit? It's exciting when someone comes to your house to play or to visit or maybe to sleep over, isn't it? Do you remember how you felt when it was time for your company to go home? How did you feel? (*Allow time for responses.*) We feel sad when our friends have to go, don't we?

In today's Gospel lesson, Jesus is saying good-bye to his friends. He has been with his disciples for three years, and now he knows he will die. How do you think Jesus was feeling as he said good-bye? (*Sad, nervous about what was going to happen, worried.*) How do you think his disciples may have been feeling? (*Probably much the same.*)

Jesus did not want to leave his disciples alone, but he knew what was going to happen. He knew that he would go to the Mount of Olives to pray, that he would be arrested, and that he would die on the cross.

Jesus was sad, and he knew his disciples were sad too. So he told them a story to help explain why he had to die.

Jesus told them to think about a seed, like this one. (*Hold up a bean seed.*) This seed is sort of dry and wrinkled. Does it look like it's alive or dead? (*Dead.*) Jesus told his disciples that a seed by itself is just a seed. But if it dries up, dies, and then is planted in the earth, it will sprout and grow. It will first get leaves, then blossoms, and, since this is a bean seed, many beans will grow from just this one seed.

Jesus was trying to tell his disciples that there was a reason he had to die. Jesus wanted them to know that when he died, he would rise again, and that because he rose from the dead, we would rise too.

How many of you have ever planted a seed? (*Allow time for responses.*) It's fun to do, and it's something everyone can learn to do. In order for a seed to grow, what do we need? (*Dirt, sun, water.*) That's right. I put some dirt in this cup. (*Show them.*) Now I will make a little hole with my finger and put the seed into it. (*Show them.*) Then I will add a little water. Not too much—just enough to keep the soil moist. Now I will need to put this seed in a sunny spot, keep watering it, and in a few days, something wonderful will happen. (*Show them the seedling.*) Out of a dried-up, wrinkled seed will come a beautiful little bean plant.

This miracle of growth reminds us that God knows how to bring life out of death. Jesus died, but God raised him up to new life. Someday we too will die, but we don't have to be sad. God will also raise us up to new life with him.   **—L.R.**

Sunday of the Passion—Palm Sunday

————————————————— • —————————————————

The Gospel: Mark 14:1—15:47

Focus: We all make mistakes, but with God's help we can start over.

Experience: The children will hear about the mistakes that Peter made. They will learn that Peter was forgiven and that he went on serving God the best way he could.

Preparation: Bring some yarn that is loosely tangled. You will need to be untangling it as you do the sermon.

God Untangles Us

(*Hold up the tangled yarn so that all may see it.*) What's wrong with this yarn? (*Allow responses.*) Yes, it is rather tangled. You can't use yarn when it is tangled. Should I throw it away, or could I do something to make it useful? (*Allow responses.*) Good idea. I think I am going to try to untangle this as we talk.

You know, sometimes our lives get tangled too. Sometimes we mean to do one thing and we end up doing just the opposite. That's what happened in the Bible story today. Jesus had a friend named Peter. When Jesus talked with Peter about some difficult times ahead, Peter said that he would always stand by Jesus, no matter what. Peter said he would even die for Jesus. At least that's what Peter *wanted* to do.

Do any of you remember what happened? (*Allow responses.*) Twice Peter made a promise he did not keep. First of all, Jesus asked Peter to wait with him in the garden while Jesus prayed. What did Peter do? (*Allow responses.*) He fell asleep several times! How do you think Peter felt? How would you feel if you fell asleep when a friend asked you to stay by him or her? (*Allow responses.*)

Later some soldiers took Jesus away. Peter followed after him. That was a brave thing to do. But then three different people said that they thought Peter was a friend of Jesus. What did Peter say? (*Allow responses.*) The same man who said he would *die* for Jesus pretended he didn't even *know* Jesus. Peter was tangled up, wasn't he?

But Peter's story doesn't end there. Instead of running away and never thinking of Jesus again, Peter stayed in the city. On Easter morning he was one of the first people to find the empty tomb. Later Peter helped lots and lots of people learn about Jesus. He ended up doing exactly what Jesus wanted him to do.

Peter got tangled up, and sometimes so do we. When we have done something wrong, God wants us to get untangled, and he will even help us. When we talk to God and say we are sorry, it is called "praying for forgiveness." After we ask God to forgive us, we can ask him to help us get untangled and start doing what he wants us to do.

(*By this point the yarn should be untangled.*) Look, my yarn is all fixed and ready to be useful again. When you get tangled up in trouble, ask God to help you get untangled. He can help you get straightened out and ready to go.   **—S.L.**

The Resurrection of Our Lord—Easter Day

The Gospel: Mark 16:1-8

Focus: Jesus' rising to life everlasting on Easter morning marked the fulfillment of God's plan of salvation.

Experience: The children will learn about the three parts most stories have, but they will find out that the story of Jesus never ends because he rose from the dead.

Preparation: Bring a storybook familiar to the children, such as *The Three Bears*.

The Story That Never Ends

Today is Easter, and as God's people we greet one another with the exciting message: he is risen! What wonderful news for all who follow Jesus and believe him to be their Lord and Savior! Did you know that the story of Jesus' life is like none other in the world? Today we will talk about why that is true.

First, however, we will talk about stories in general. I have here a simple story *The Three Bears*. (*Hold up book.*) Like most other stories, it has three main parts. The first part is the beginning, where we usually meet the characters. The second part is the middle, where much of the action takes place. Finally, we have the conclusion, where the problem is solved or we find out how the story turns out.

A person's life could be compared to those three parts of a story. What do we call it when people begin their life? (*Their birth.*) That's right. Jesus Christ was born, just as you and I were born.

As people grow, many things happen in their lives. This is like the middle of a story. Many important things happened to Jesus, especially during his ministry. We read all about the events of Jesus' life in the Bible.

All stories have a conclusion, an end. What do we usually call the end of a person's life? (*Death.*) That's right. We call the end of a person's life, death. We might say that when a person dies, it is like the end of a story. Did Jesus die? (*Yes.*) Yes, he did. But was death the end of the story of Jesus? (*No.*) No, it wasn't, because on that first Easter morning, Christ rose from the dead. He is alive and will never die again.

The story of Jesus is very different from other stories. Even though Jesus died, that was not the end of the story. Jesus' story is a story that never ends. He is alive! He will live forever.

We will all die someday, but the Bible tells us that death is not the end of our story either. The Bible says that whoever believes in Jesus will be raised to live with him in heaven forever.

Let's share this story that never ends with others today. (*Address the congregation.*) We will say the words *Christ is risen!* You can say back to us "Christ is risen indeed!" (*Lead the children in saying the phrase and indicate when the congregation should respond.*) Let's share the story!   **—D.H.**

Second Sunday of Easter

— • —

The Gospel: John 20:19-31

Focus: God uses what we can see to help us believe in what we cannot see.

Experience: The children will have a chance to test the phrase, *seeing is believing.*

Preparation: Bring either a dollar bill, folded small enough to fit in the palm of your hand, or a silver dollar.

Believing without Seeing

I would like all of you to look at my hand. (*Hold your hand up in front of you with your fist clenched and the back of your hand toward the children.*) Would you believe me if I told you that I had a dollar in my hand? (*Allow time for responses.*) I noticed that while some of you were saying there is a dollar in my hand, a few of you weren't sure. What could I do to get all of you to believe that I do have a dollar in my hand? (*Allow time for responses.*) You are correct. If I open my hand, we will all know if I have a dollar in it or not. (*Open your hand and show that, indeed, there is a dollar there.*)

This reminds me of a saying I have heard: seeing is believing. In our Gospel lesson for today Jesus' friends—the disciples—were convinced that Jesus was alive when they saw him standing before them. Not all of the disciples were present, however, when Jesus appeared. Thomas was not with them. When the other disciples told Thomas that they had seen Jesus, he couldn't believe it. He needed proof. Guess what Thomas wanted to do before he would believe? (*Allow time for responses.*) Yes. Thomas wanted to see Jesus as the other disciples had.

Jesus said something quite interesting to Thomas immediately after Thomas saw him. He said, "Have you believed because you have seen me? Blessed are those who have not seen and yet have come to believe" (v. 29).

How many of you believe in Jesus? (*Allow time for responses.*) How many of you have seen Jesus in person? (*Allow time for responses.*) Then Jesus' words to Thomas are for us too! Jesus was talking about us and everyone who believes in him without seeing him. We have a word to describe believing without seeing. That word is *faith*.

We believe in Jesus as our Lord and Savior, not because we can see him with our eyes but because we can trust him with our hearts. Through the power of the Holy Spirit, God uses things we can see to help us believe in what we cannot see. As we hear of God's great love for us in sending his Son Jesus to live, die, and rise again for our salvation, we believe. As we see God's love at work in our friends, our family, and our church, we believe. Yes, we are the ones that Jesus meant when he said, "Blessed are those who have not seen and yet have come to believe."   **—D.H.**

Third Sunday of Easter

———————————————— • ————————————————

The Gospel: Luke 24:36-49

Focus: Jesus helped the disciples to understand Scripture, and he sends the Holy Spirit to help us do the same.

Experience: The children will meet three people and decide how they can help us learn. The children will also hear about the Holy Spirit, the helper Jesus sent.

Preparation: Obtain the following props and enlist the aid of youth or older children to play the following roles: a carpenter wearing safety glasses and carrying a hammer, a coach wearing a whistle around the neck, a letter jacket or ball cap, and sneakers; a musician carrying some sheet music and a musical instrument.

Teachers

When I was little, I used to ask lots of questions. Asking questions was a very good way to learn about things I did not understand.

Do you ever have questions? (*Allow responses.*) Who are some people you go to when you have questions? (*Parents, teacher, pastor, adults, friends, expert.*) God provides us with special people in our lives to help us understand many things.

(*Have your three volunteers come forward and stand where all the children can see them.*) Here are three helpers. I would like you to pick out the best person to help with certain activities.

It's lots of fun to play baseball. Of the three people standing here which one do you think could best help us learn how to play baseball? (*Allow responses.*) That is correct. This person is willing to help others to learn about baseball. What do we call someone who teaches others how to play a sport? (*Coach.*) That's right.

How many of you enjoy listening to music? (*Allow responses.*) So do I. I particularly enjoy listening to someone playing a musical instrument. If I wanted to learn how to play an instrument, which of these people could be of the greatest help to me? (*Allow responses.*) Yes. The music teacher not only knows how to play several musical instruments but also can teach others so they understand how to do it as well.

How many of you like to make things? (*Allow responses.*) I always wish I knew how to build things — maybe to make a bookshelf or a birdhouse. A person like this one (*point to the carpenter*) knows how to build things. This is a carpenter.

In our Gospel for today the disciples were confused by the things that had happened to Jesus. He had been beaten, crucified, buried, and now they were hearing that he was alive. Jesus came to them, showed them that he was truly alive, and then helped them to understand the Scriptures. Then Jesus made a special promise. He told them he would send them a special helper to keep them strong in their faith and give them power to share the story of his love with others. That helper is the Holy Spirit.

God uses special people today to help us understand the Bible too. Who are some of them? (*Help the children to see that pastors, Sunday school teachers, family, friends, youth ministers, and others help us to understand the Bible and grow in faith.*) As these people share with us what they know, that special helper, the Holy Spirit, gives us faith and helps our faith to grow. The Holy Spirit helps us to believe that Jesus is our Lord and Savior.   **—D.H.**

Fourth Sunday of Easter

————————————•————————————

The Gospel: John 10:11-18

Focus: Jesus demonstrated through his life of service that he is truly the good shepherd.

Experience: The children will learn that "good" is what someone *does*, not just what that person *says*, and that Jesus is our good shepherd because he gave his life for us.

Preparation: Bring a piece of athletic equipment (*baseball glove, golf club, etc.*). If there are artists, writers, or composers in your congregation or family, have a sample of their work on hand.

The Good Shepherd

(*Begin by walking out with a baseball glove on your hand.*) Do you know what this is? (*Allow responses.*) That's right. It is a baseball glove. In fact, it is my glove. Would you believe me if I told you that I was a good baseball player? (*Expect a mixture of answers and ask the children why they answered as they did.*)

How could you find out whether or not I am a good baseball player? (*Allow responses.*) OK, we could play baseball, and the way I hit, run, and throw would tell you whether I was a good player.

The point I am trying to make is simply this: *good* is what you do, not just what you say.

In our text for today Jesus calls himself the good shepherd. He goes on to tell us that the good shepherd lays down his life for the sheep. If Jesus is the shepherd, who are the sheep? (*We are.*) That's right. We are like sheep who follow Jesus and listen to him. We are like sheep who need a shepherd to care for us and protect us.

A shepherd who was doing his job would give up his life to save his sheep. Jesus loves us and died for us.

So, how do we know that Jesus is our good shepherd? We know because Jesus told us so, but we also know because Jesus has shown us that he loves us.   **—D.H.**

Fifth Sunday of Easter

————————————— • —————————————

The Gospel: John 15:1-8

Focus: We become connected to Christ as the Holy Spirit, working through the Word helps us to believe and trust in Jesus as our Savior.

Experience: Involve some children to simulate a vine with many branches. They will be asked to portray a vine with healthy branches and then demonstrate what happens to a branch that is broken off from the vine.

The Vine and the Branches

Spring is a special time of the year. The trees and other plants blossom and grow as God sends rain and warm sunshine their way. What does a healthy plant, like a tree, look like in the spring as it awakens from its winter sleep and begins to grow? (*First it is bare, then buds, blossoms, and leaves appear.*)

Let's work together to show what a plant looks like. I need one person to be the vine. (*Select a volunteer and have that child stand.*) Now I need four people to be branches. (*Select four children. Have two children join hands and one pair stand on each side of the "vine." Then have each "branch" join hands with the "vine."*) Great! Now, the rest of us will be the weather. Let's make some sunshine to help the plant grow. (*Pantomime the sun in the sky.*) Now let's have some rain. (*Pantomime rainfall.*) The tree will grow as long as it has both rain and sun, right? (*Yes.*)

What will happen, however, if one of the branches is broken off the vine? (*Have one of the younger children let go of the older child and show what will happen. Prompt the children to curl up and sit down.*) Unlike all the other branches that are still connected to the vine, this branch will soon wither and die. Even if the sun shines and the rain falls, will this branch live? (*No.*) Why? (*It's not connected to the vine.*) Right. If the branch is not connected to the vine, it cannot live or grow.

In our Gospel lesson for today Jesus tells us that he is the vine and we are the branches. Jesus is saying that he wants us to be as close to him as branches are to a vine. That is how we grow as children of God.

How do we stay close to Jesus? The Holy Spirit gives us faith and helps us to grow. Who are some people who help our faith to grow? (*Affirm all answers.*) That's right. People can listen to our questions and help us to learn about Jesus. Do you know what else? You can help other people grow in their faith too. When we pray together, worship together, study the Bible together, sing together, play together—all these are times when we can tell others about Jesus and his love.

So let's remember: our faith is a gift from God, and just as a branch grows when it is connected to a tree, our faith grows when we stay connected to Jesus.   **—D.H.**

Sixth Sunday of Easter

—————————————— • ——————————————

The Gospel: John 15:9-17

Focus: Jesus not only told his disciples what to do but also gave them a standard by which to measure their love. He said, "Love one another as I have loved you."

Experience: By paraphrasing Jesus' words from today's Gospel, you and the children will share this truth—"This is what I (Jesus) want(s) you to do: love one another as I have loved you."

Love As I Have Loved

Jesus told his friends, the disciples, many important truths while he was with them. One of the commands he gave them he repeated several times. He said, "Love one another." We know this was important to Jesus, not only because he repeated it several times but because he called it a commandment, something he wanted them to do. How were they to love one another?

Before we answer that question, I would like for you to join me in a rhyming game. The game is called, "This Is What I Want You to Do."

Let's begin. This is what I want you to do: put one hand on your head and the other on your shoe. (*Allow time for response.*) You certainly didn't have any trouble with that.

This is what I want you to do: stand up tall if you are wearing something blue. (*Allow time for response.*) You had to think a little about that one, didn't you?

This is what I want you to do: pretend you have to sneeze and say ach-choo. (*Allow time for response.*) Bless you!

This is what I want you to do: give a gentle hug to someone next to you. (*Allow time for response.*) Thank you!

This is what I want you to do: stand and say "hurray" if you're a Christian too. (*Allow time for response.*) Great!

Now let's talk about Jesus' commandment to his disciples—what he wanted them to do. He said, "Love one another." Jesus didn't just tell them what he wanted them to do. He also told them how they were to do it. He said, "This is what I want you to do: love one another as I have loved you." How did Jesus love us? (*He loved and cared so much for us that he was willing to die for us. He taught people. He fed people. He healed people.*) Now Jesus wants us to be as loving and concerned for one another as he is for us. How can we show love for one another? (*Affirm responses. If they can't think of any, suggest opportunities available locally: food shelf, playing with a sad child, sharing toys, passing on outgrown clothing, giving offering to church, and so on.*)

Jesus says to all of us, "This is what I want you to do: love one another as I have loved you." Let's say that together. (*Love one another as I have loved you.*)   **—D.H.**

Seventh Sunday of Easter
———————————————— • ————————————————

The Gospel: John 17:11b-19

Focus: Jesus sanctifies believers—makes them holy—for a purpose: so they might share the good news with others.

Experience: You will illustrate through several examples that certain items are made for a specific purpose. You will teach that we too as redeemed children of God are made holy for a purpose. That purpose is to share the Gospel message with those who don't know Jesus.

Preparation: Bring some common objects such as a glass pitcher, a hammer, and a pair of sunglasses. Be sure to bring a Bible as part of your collection of items (the Bible will be the last item you use).

Holy for a Purpose

In our Gospel lesson for today, we find Jesus doing something he did often: praying. It was nearly time for him to die on the cross, and he knew that the disciples would need help to do God's work on earth. For that reason Jesus asked his heavenly Father to "sanctify" his disciples—that means to make them holy, set apart for a special purpose.

Everything has a purpose, a special reason, a job to do.

(*Pick up the empty glass pitcher and ask the children to identify it.*) This is an item we normally find in what room of the house? (*Allow responses.*) Yes. What do we use pitchers for? (*Allow responses.*) Yes, the pitcher is a container for holding liquids like water, Kool-Aid, tea, and so on. If the pitcher isn't used for holding liquids, is it serving the purpose for which it was made? (*No.*)

(*Next show the children the hammer and ask the children to identify it.*) Where do we normally keep a hammer? (*Allow responses.*) Yes. What can you do with a hammer? (*Allow responses.*) Yes, the hammer is used to drive in or remove nails. If the hammer stays in my toolbox and is never used to drive in or remove nails, is it serving the purpose for which it was made? (*No.*)

(*Hold up the pair of sunglasses and ask the children to identify them.*) Where do you usually use sunglasses? (*Allow responses.*) Right. Why do you need sunglasses? (*Allow responses.*) That's right. We use sunglasses to protect our eyes from the bright rays of the sun. If I left these sunglasses at home on my desk and never wore them, would they be serving the purpose for which they were made? (*No.*)

Jesus loved his friends, and he knew they would need help to do the special work God wanted them to do. Jesus asked his heavenly Father to take care of his friends, the disciples. He asked that God would protect them from the devil. He also asked God to sanctify the disciples. Remember that to *sanctify* them means to make them holy or to give them a special job to do. How would God do that? What would God use to make the disciples holy? God had a special tool to make the disciples holy, and it was this (*hold up the Holy Bible*). The disciples didn't have a Bible like this one. But they heard the words Jesus spoke, and they remembered them. The Holy Spirit used these words to help the disciples believe in Jesus as their Savior.

Why do you think Jesus wanted to make them holy? He had a very special purpose for them. In his prayer to God he said, "As you have sent me into the world, so I have sent them into the world." That is the reason he made them holy—so that they could share the good news of Jesus with others.

Jesus used his Word to make the disciples holy. He still uses his Word to make us holy so we can go tell others about Jesus and his love.   **—D.H.**

The Day of Pentecost

——————————— • ———————————

The Gospel: John 7:37-39a

Focus: Jesus is the source for anyone who is "thirsty for God" (needs God and his love). He promises to give us the Holy Spirit who will strengthen our faith and help us to share the good news with others.

Experience: This message will lead the children through a series of physical needs and conclude by pointing to Jesus as the source for satisfying our "thirst for God."

Thirsty for God

God has blessed us with wonderful bodies. Sometimes our bodies let us know when they have needs. How many of you have ever been thirsty? (*Allow responses.*) What did you need when you were thirsty? (*Allow responses.*) That's right. You could best satisfy your body's thirst by drinking something. Have any of you ever been really hungry? (*Allow responses.*) What did your body need to make that hungry feeling go away? (*Allow responses.*) Yes. You needed some food to eat.

We have talked about the needs that our bodies have. What Jesus was talking about in our Gospel lesson for today is a need that we all have in our hearts and souls. When he said, "If you are thirsty . . . ", he meant "If you need to know about God, then come to me." We all need to know about God's great love for us. Who do we need? Who did Jesus say we should come to? (*Allow responses.*) Yes, Jesus said we should come to him. He promises us not only the forgiveness of our sins but also a very special gift. That gift is the Holy Spirit.

The Holy Spirit fills us with the love of God so that we want to tell others about God's love for us in Jesus Christ. The Holy Spirit stays in our hearts and daily reminds us of God's love for us in Christ Jesus.

What wonderful bodies God has given us. They alert us when they have needs so we can do what's necessary to take care of them. What a wonderful gift God has given us in his Son, Jesus Christ, who lived, died, and rose again for our salvation. Finally, thank God for the wonderful gift of the Holy Spirit, who not only helps us to believe and keeps us in the faith but also strengthens us to share the good news with others. **—D.H.**

The Holy Trinity—First Sunday after Pentecost

—————————————————— • ——————————————————

The Gospel: John 3:1-17

Focus: The Trinity is three in one.

Experience: You will show the children two examples of things that are three yet one.

Preparation: Bring enough three-looped pretzels (sometimes called "knots") to give one to each child. (Do not get pretzel sticks!)

The Trinity

How many of you like pretzels? (*Hold one up.*) Me, too.

Did you know that the recipe for pretzels is very, very old? They have been made for over 1500 years! About 600 years after Jesus' times a monk was playing with some leftover bread dough, making different shapes with thin strips of it. He found that when he folded the ends over each other, and then up, the shape looked a little like someone praying. (*Fold your arms so that they cross your chest with the fingers of your right hand resting on your left shoulder and the fingers of your left hand touching your right shoulder.*) Do I look like a pretzel? Well, he thought the loops looked like the arms and head of someone praying. (*Hold pretzel so the single loop, representing the head, is at the top. Then trace the loops.*) The monk named his creation *pretiola*, which meant "little reward" in Latin, and he gave them to boys and girls as a little reward for learning their prayers well. The children liked them, just as we do.

I was looking at a pretzel last night. This pretzel is one pretzel, made of one strip of dough, but it has three separate loops. It made me think of the Trinity. We say there's one God but that God is in three persons: God the Father, God the Son, and God the Holy Spirit. That's hard to understand! How can there be one God, and yet be three persons?

Well—one pretzel, three loops.

Or, consider the room we're sitting in. This is one room, but it has three dimensions. There's the height: the distance from the ceiling to the floor (*demonstrate with your hands held apart vertically*); there's the width: the distance from side to side (*hold hands apart horizontally*); and there's the length: the distance from front to back (*hold hands apart, one in front of the other*). You can't take away any one of those dimensions and still have a room left. If you take away the height, you'll be left with just a floor (*once more, hold hands apart vertically, and then bring them together to demonstrate the loss of height. Do the same for the other two dimensions.*) Take away the width, or the length, and you'll be left with a wall. The room is gone. In the same way, if you break off one of the loops of the pretzel, it's no longer a whole pretzel but a piece.

So we have one God but three persons in that God. We have God the Father (*hold up your pretzel and trace one loop*), who created the world and everything in it, including us. We have God the Son, Jesus (*trace another loop*), whom God sent to teach us what he's like and what he wants us to do. Jesus died on the cross for us and rose up to live with God eternally. We have God the Holy Spirit (*trace third loop*), who guides us and helps us. The Holy Spirit helps us to know Jesus better and draws us closer to God.

One room, three dimensions; one pretzel, three loops; one God, three persons: (*trace the loops again*) Father, Son, and Holy Spirit. Today is Trinity Sunday, when we celebrate that three-in-one nature of God.

Now, before you return to your seats, I have something for each of you to remind you of God, the three in one. (*Distribute pretzels.*)

—L.W.

Second Sunday after Pentecost

————————————— • —————————————

The Gospel: Mark 2:23-28

Focus: The Pharisees loved the law, but Jesus loved people.

Experience: You will give the children several examples of Jesus' breaking the rules when necessary so he could help someone.

Simon Says

Sometimes I think there are a lot of rules we have to follow. Can you think of some rules? (*Stop for a red light. Don't steal. Eat with your fork. Wear clothes.*) We have rules to follow at home and rules to follow at school.

Even games have rules to follow. Take "Simon Says," for example. I tell you to do certain things. The rule is, you do those things only if I say "Simon says" first. If I don't say "Simon says," then you shouldn't follow my directions.

Let's play a short game of Simon Says right now. Simon says stand up. Simon says touch your head. Touch your knees. Uh-oh. I didn't say "Simon says." Your hands should be on your heads, not your knees. Simon says turn around. Simon says touch your toes. Simon says reach way up! Now clap two times. Uh-oh. Simon didn't say to clap! OK, Simon says sit down.

Jesus knew about rules. Whole books of the Old Testament listed all the rules Jesus was expected to follow. However, Jesus didn't always follow them. He knew that people were more important than rules. If he had to choose between helping someone and obeying the law, Jesus would choose the person over the law.

For example, one major rule was that people shouldn't work on the Sabbath. They were to spend the day praying, worshiping, and thinking about God. They were to set the day apart for those activities by not working. That sounds like a good idea, doesn't it? But Jesus got into trouble over that rule a lot. He and his disciples picked grain on the Sabbath when they were hungry. Jesus healed one man who couldn't walk, one who couldn't see, and another who had a withered hand. These healings all took place on the Sabbath. Healing was considered to be work, so Jesus had broken the rule. The rules said, "Don't heal them; that's work." But Jesus said, "It is possible to honor God and still work on the Sabbath. I'll heal them because God loves them."

Another rule was, don't mix with "bad" people, such as tax collectors, sinners, and Gentiles. Show that you're better than they are by refusing to have anything to do with them. Jesus ate with such people, talked with them, befriended them, and healed them. The rules said, "Ignore them! Hate them!" But Jesus said, "They are God's people too. They need me just as sick people need doctors. I love them."

The Pharisees got very angry with Jesus. They believed that the way to please God was to follow all these rules. They didn't like what Jesus did. However, Jesus knew he was pleasing God by showing God's love to others. For Jesus, people mattered more than rules. Jesus listened to God. His rule said, "Love one another."

—L.W.

Third Sunday after Pentecost

————————————————————•————————————————————

The Gospel: Mark 3:20-35

Focus: When we do God's will, Jesus says we are more than followers. We are his brothers and sisters.

Experience: You will teach that if Jesus is our brother, then we are all members of God's family and children of the King.

Preparation: You will need a crown for each child. You might be able to get them from a fast-food restaurant or you could make your own. If you have the time and talent, you could make them with the children.

God's Family

Let's conduct a little survey. Raise your hand if you have a pet. Raise your hand if you have a bicycle. Raise your hand if you have a brother or sister. Wow, a lot of you do! (*Ask one child*), Who's your brother (*or sister*)? (*Response.*) That means the two of you belong to the same family, right? (*Ask a few more children the same question. Emphasize family, but remember that you cannot assume that all brothers and sisters have the same parents.*)

It's nice to be part of a family. A family shares a special closeness. You share a lot of the same experiences. You have memories and history in common. Friends may move away or forget about you, but you're always related to your family.

I love my family, but I must admit I have always enjoyed stories about kings and queens. I always kind of dreamed about being the child of a king. If you had a king for your father, what would your life be like? (*Affirm responses.*) That's right. I thought I would be able to wear fancy clothes and a crown. I thought I could have a beautiful pony. I *really* wanted a pony! It sounded great!

Well, guess what. I *do* have a king for a father. In fact, so do you. (*Give out crowns.*) In the Bible Jesus said that anyone who did the will of God was his—Jesus'—brother and sister. If we are Jesus' brothers and sisters, then we are family. We have the same Father as he has. So who's our Father? (*God.*) And God is King! His kingdom is heaven. So wear your crown with pride! You are a child of the King!

—L.W.

Fourth Sunday after Pentecost
—————————————————— • ——————————————————

The Gospel: Mark 4:26-34

Focus: God can use the little things we do for his kingdom.

Experience: Jesus compared the kingdom of heaven to a mustard seed. Children understand that little seeds grow into large plants. By analogy they will see that God uses little things we can do for him to his glory and purpose.

Preparation: Bring a variety of seeds, and perhaps the plant or fruit the seed produces, to show the children. An apple or tomato you can cut open to display the seeds inside is a definite plus.

The Mustard Seed

I love working in my garden. I enjoy seeing lovely flowers and fresh vegetables grow from the seeds I have planted in the spring. It amazes me that a tiny seed will produce a big plant without much help from me. I brought in some seeds to show you. (*These may be on a plate or glued to a plain piece of cardboard. Try to show some of various sizes and shapes. Point them out or pass them around as you talk about them. Describe what each seed will become. Ask the children if they like the different vegetables or flowers.*)

There's a lot of variety in the seeds themselves and, of course, in the plants they came from. Some are big. Some are small. But all seeds, to me, are miraculous.

(*Choose one little vegetable seed.*) Look at these little seeds. If I put one in the ground and water it and let God's sunshine warm it, do you know what will happen? (*It will grow.*) Yes, it will grow into a big plant. (*Describe what this particular plant will look like and what sort of food it will produce. If possible, show more seeds inside the fruit.*)

I plant the seed, but I don't pull the stem to make the plant grow or paste the flowers on or stuff seeds into the fruit. God has it all worked out so that the plant does it all on its own. Inside each tiny seed there's everything it needs to grow and blossom and produce more seeds. Incredible, isn't it?

Jesus said that the kingdom of heaven is like a seed—a mustard seed. The seed itself is tiny, but Jesus said birds could nest in the full-grown plant.

That also applies to us. When we do something good, our little act of kindness may seem to be as tiny as a seed. Somehow, though, God can take our small deed or gift and make it grow and blossom and bear fruit for his kingdom.

Maybe one of you visited someone in a care center, and you stopped and picked up a book that a woman in a wheelchair had accidentally dropped. You smiled at each other. Later you saw she was smiling at other people and they were smiling too. So your little act of kindness spread happiness to many people.

I don't know how God makes good deeds grow any more than I can explain how a tomato seed is able to produce other tomatoes. Maybe it's because, even though we and our actions seem small, God, who made us, is powerful and wise. Truly, God can do marvelous things!   **—L.W.**

Fifth Sunday after Pentecost

———————————— • ————————————

The Gospel: Mark 4:35-41

Focus: Jesus is Lord over nature.

Experience: You will do something "magical." The children should be surprised and impressed. As you act out the story, you will relate the children's reactions to the reactions of the disciples when Jesus calmed the storm.

Preparation: You want to be able to do something the children cannot do and to accomplish it by apparently supernatural means. I use turning out a light because in my church the light switches are in the back, and an usher can hit the switch without being seen. If you can't think of a feat to do, skip the introduction and go straight to acting out the story.

Jesus, the Master

We're going to try an experiment this morning. I'm going to test you for magic powers. Let's see if you can turn off this light, using only the power of your mind. (*If your group is too large to call on each child individually, you can have them try in groups of five, or all the boys and then all the girls, or by rows. The light, of course, should go off only for you.*)

Here we go. Each of you concentrate hard on making the light go off. (*Give everyone a chance.*) Nobody had any success at all. Now it's my turn. (*Point to the light, or say, "Light, go off!" The usher turns it off promptly on your signal.*)

Did that surprise you? (*Let them answer.*) Did it scare you a little bit? (*They respond.*) Well, I have to confess that the usher turned the light off for me. I don't really have any special powers.

Jesus did, though. Today's Gospel lesson tells about a time when Jesus used his power to do something none of his disciples could do. We're going to pretend we're all Jesus' disciples. (*Ask for a volunteer.*) You'll be Jesus. Before we get into the boat, let's get ready for the storm. When I talk about the wind, let's all make the sound of wind. Let's practice! I want to hear all of you. (*Practice blowing out. Don't let them get too loud.*) When the waves got big, the boat tossed about. Let's pretend: lean from side to side (*demon-*

strate). Rowing the boat goes like this (*demonstrate*), and bailing out the water looks like this (*demonstrate*). OK, I think we're ready.

Now, it happened that Jesus and his disciples decided to go out in a boat. Let's all get in the boat (*rearrange them, if necessary, so they're all facing the same way and so there's room for the child who will be Jesus to sit behind them*). Jesus was very tired, so he got in the back and fell asleep (*have the volunteer lie down behind the other children*). Let's start rowing across the sea. (*Pantomime rowing for a little while.*) As the disciples went along, the wind began to blow. (*Lead them in making soft wind noises.*) The wind made the waves rough, and the boat began to rock. (*All lean from side to side.*) The boat began to take on water. We'd better bail! (*Do so.*) The wind blew very hard (*make louder wind noises*), and the waves got big. The disciples were scared! They were afraid the boat would tip over or sink. The wind blew harder. (*Make louder wind noises and keep them going until Jesus stills the storm.*) Bail faster! (*Pantomime.*) Can we call the Coast Guard for help? Oh, dear! Should we swim for shore? We're very far out. What should we do? (*Let them make suggestions.*)

Somebody, wake up Jesus. (*Ask for a volunteer.*) Wake up Jesus and tell him we're in trouble. (*Help the children act out the story.*) Say, "Don't you care if we drown?" (*Allow volunteer to repeat this phrase.*) Jesus wasn't scared. He said, "Wind, be quiet!" (*Jesus says this and you stop making wind noises.*) He told the waves, "Peace; be still." (*He does. Stop rocking the boat.*) OK! We can bail out the boat and we'll be safe. (*Thank the volunteers and have them sit with the rest.*)

Wow! That was exciting, wasn't it! The storm had terrified the disciples. I'm sure they were relieved when Jesus stopped the wind and calmed the waves. But it was kind of scary, too. Think about how you felt when I turned off the light. The disciples were amazed! They asked each other, "Who then is this, that even wind and the sea obey him?"

They knew it was Jesus. But they were amazed at his power. Jesus, who is master of the wind and waves, is the same Jesus who loved us enough to die for us. He is always with us, even when we're frightened or in trouble. Jesus is our Lord, our Savior, our Friend.

—L.W.

Sixth Sunday after Pentecost

—————————————————— • ——————————————————

The Gospel: Mark 5:21-43

Focus: Jesus healed people with the power of love.

Experience: You and the children will compare present-day medicine and Jesus' way of healing.

Preparation: Bring a tray on which you display plastic bandages, antiseptic, an athletic bandage, cough syrup, pills, a syringe from a child's medicine play kit, and a magic wand. Wear a plastic bandage yourself in a conspicuous place.

The Power of Love

I cut myself yesterday. I put a bandage on it (*show it*), but it still hurts a little. When you get a cut or scrape your knee, how do you take care of it? (*Let them answer.*)

How about when you get sick? (*Indicate tray.*) I have some of the things the doctor might use to help you when you're sick. Let's see . . . when you have a cough, does the doctor use these? (*Hold up plastic bandages.*) How about this? (*Hold up cough syrup.*) For chicken pox would the doctor use this (*athletic bandage*), or this (*syringe*)? Probably neither one. OK, if you had a tummy ache, would the doctor use this? (*Show magic wand.*) No? How about this (*antiseptic*)? Well, depending on what your sickness is, the doctor can use these items to help you get better.

Jesus could cure people without using any of these. Once he was asked to go heal a young girl. A big crowd walked along with him to watch him and listen to him. Among these people was a woman who had been sick for twelve years. Twelve years! That's a long time. Some of you aren't even twelve years old yet. This woman had been to doctors, but she was still sick.

She had heard about Jesus. She said to herself, "I won't bother him. I'm a little afraid to ask him to help me. But I think if I could just touch his robe, I could be healed." So she managed to get close enough to reach out her hand, and she touched his robe. Just one light touch, and immediately she was well! That's all it took.

Even though she had only touched his robe, Jesus knew that

something had happened. He stopped. "Who touched me?" he asked.

There were people all around Jesus. The disciples said, "Oh, come on. Look at all these people! What do you mean, who touched you?" But Jesus insisted that someone had touched him. He had felt power go out from him. "Who touched me?" he asked again.

The woman was frightened. She was scared that he might be angry. Trembling, she came forward and confessed that she had touched him in order to be healed. I can picture Jesus smiling tenderly at her. He wasn't mad! "Daughter," he said, "your faith has made you well." Then he went on to take care of the little girl.

What power Jesus had, that this woman could be healed just by touching his robe! He didn't need any of the things I have on my tray (*indicate*). He used a tremendous power. And do you know what it was called? (*Allow responses and affirm what you hear, but encourage them to name the power of love.*) Jesus used the most powerful thing in the world—the power of his love. And he has given us this power too. Jesus tells us, "Love one another as I have loved you."

We may not be able to heal people with our love, as Jesus did, but we can help them in many ways. Today, I hope you will find a way to share God's love with others.   **—L.W.**

Seventh Sunday after Pentecost
———————————•———————————

The Gospel: Mark 6:1-6

Focus: Jesus never forces people to believe in him. Rather, he invites us.

Experience: The children will see that even people they think they know fairly well can have hidden talents they know nothing about. Similarly, Jesus was scorned by people in his home town because they didn't know who he was.

Preparation: Find people among the congregation whom the children know—the organist, Sunday school teachers, parents, choir members, and others—who have some special talent the children are not likely to know about. There should be some tangible evidence of this talent which you can display: a trophy, a painting, an award, a demonstration of a talent, some piece of handiwork, and so on. You can display the talent up front and point out the appropriate item when you mention the person, or have the person demonstrate the talent when you call upon him or her.

An alternate introduction would be to think up some brief activity for the children, such as changing positions or sampling a snack you've prepared. *Invite* the first bunch of kids to do the activity, but *command* the second batch to do it. Compare the two approaches. They should find being invited preferable to being ordered to do it. Proceed to the second paragraph.

We Are Invited

Our congregation has a lot of special people. You may think you know them, but I think they may surprise you. For instance, here is *(name)*, and you know he plays the organ, but did you know he also *(Tell about his hidden talent)*. *(Introduce the people and their talents, one by one. Thank them for sharing their talents.)* Maybe you didn't know these people were so talented!

The people in Jesus' home town thought they knew him well. After all, it was a small town. They knew Joseph, his father, was a carpenter, and they knew his mother, Mary, seemed to be an ordinary woman.

But when Jesus came home and preached, they couldn't believe what they heard. They said, "We know him! He's no big deal—just the son of a carpenter. How did he get to be so smart? Who does he think he is, anyway?" They didn't know he was the Son of God.

Jesus could easily have *made* them realize who he was. He could have done miracles and wonders to impress them. He could have said, "OK, you don't believe in me? Watch this!" Then he could have uprooted big trees or caused a mountain to disappear. But that's not Jesus' style.

Jesus never forces us to believe in him. Rather, he *invites* us to believe. There's a verse in the Bible that says, "Listen! I am standing at the door, knocking; if you hear my voice and open the door, I will come in" (Revelation 3:20). It's our choice whether to open the door or not. He knocks and waits.

Jesus doesn't grab us by the shoulders and say, "You have to believe in me! I *demand* that you believe in me!" He invites us. When we open the door and say, "Come in," Jesus will greet us with open arms. Remember today that Jesus loves you and is waiting for you to invite him into your life.   **—L.W.**

Eighth Sunday after Pentecost

———————————————— • ————————————————

The Gospel: Mark 6:7-13

Focus: In today's Gospel, Jesus sent the disciples to do mission work. Likewise, we are sent.

Experience: Talk with the children about Jesus sending us on a mission. Then let the children come up with a list of things that we can do to fulfill our mission.

Preparation: You will need poster board and a marker.

Sent on a Mission

I used to love to watch movies about spies and secret agents. Do you ever watch movies like that? The spy would be sent on a mission. The general would walk in and say, "I have a mission for you. Your mission is to rescue one of our agents who is being held prisoner by our enemies." Then the spy would go out and do the mission.

I always thought it would be exciting to be sent on a mission. Does that sound exciting to you? (*Accept responses.*)

Well, guess what the Bible tells us? *We* are sent out on a mission! We aren't spies or secret agents, but Jesus does send us on a mission. And our mission is to tell all the world about Jesus. That's what we as Christians are to do.

But you know, that makes me wonder. If our mission is to tell people about Jesus, how do we do that?

Let's see if we can figure out some ways to do our mission. I'm going to ask you to tell me your ideas about how we can do our mission and I'll write them down. Let's see what kind of a list we can come up with.

So tell me, what are some ways that we can tell the world about Jesus? (*Allow time for the children to think and respond. Be sure to affirm the responses that are given. For example, we can invite people to church, pray, help people, give offerings, or tell people about Jesus. You should record their responses.*)

That looks like a good list. Let's see what we've written. (*Review the list.*) Those are all ways that we can do our mission.

But I wonder, do we go on our mission all alone? (*No.*) Who goes with us? (*Friends, family, other Christians, the church, and most importantly, God. Help the children to realize that sometimes they may feel as though they're all alone, but God is always with them.*) That's right! Sometimes we go with partners, sometimes we go alone, but always God goes with us.

Please remember, we are sent on a mission. We may not be spies, we may not be secret agents, but we are Christians, and that's even more exciting! Our mission is to tell the world about Jesus.   **—M.B.**

Ninth Sunday after Pentecost
—————————————— • ——————————————

The Gospel: Mark 6:30-34

Focus: Today's Gospel tells us of Jesus' compassion and care for people. This sermon will help each child to realize that he or she is a person cared for by Jesus and that Jesus cares for all people.

Experience: Tell the children you will divide them into two groups. One group will be for the children that Jesus loves, and the other group will be children that Jesus doesn't care about. Then place all children in the first group.

Preparation: Bring a Bible and a piece of paper. On the paper have these words written: "Jesus loves all children and all other people." If you want accompaniment, be sure to alert the organist that at the end of the sermon you will have the congregation join with the children in singing "Jesus Loves Me."

Jesus Loves Us All

We are always talking about Jesus and his love, so I thought today I'd try to figure out who are the people that Jesus *really* cares about. I decided to start with you children. I knew we'd be talking together this morning, so I thought we'd try to figure out which of you Jesus thinks is special.

What I did was read through the Bible to see what it could tell me. (*Hold up the Bible.*) Based on the Bible, I've made some notes. (*Hold up the paper.*)

So, what I'm going to do is divide you into two groups. On my right side (*point with your right hand*) I'm going to place all the children that Jesus loves. On my left side (*point with your left hand*), I'm going to put all the children that Jesus doesn't care about. Let's give it a try.

Here we go. We'll start with you. (*Look at your notes.*) Congratulations, Jesus loves you! Please sit over there to my right. (*Have the child walk over and sit off to your right.*)

(*Look at the list again and continue until you have seated all the children to your right. You may seat them in small groups if your group is large, for example, "Everyone with brown eyes," and so on.*)

(*Turn and face all the children.*) Well, it looks like you are all over here. And that's right. You are all children that Jesus loves. That's what my list says. It says, "Jesus loves all children and all people." (*Show the children the piece of paper.*) And the Bible tells us that Jesus cares very much for each and every one of you. That's the wonderful thing that we know as Christians. Jesus loves us. That's something for us to remember today and every day.

I'd like for us to close by singing a song. Let's sing "Jesus Loves Me." (*You may have accompaniment or could have the whole congregation sing with you.*) And as we sing, remember that you are a person that Jesus loves!

—M.B.

Tenth Sunday after Pentecost

———————————— • ————————————

The Gospel: John 6:1-15

Focus: The children will examine the story of Jesus feeding over 5000 people.

Experience: The children will help to write a newspaper that tells about Jesus' miracle. In doing so they will become more familiar with the story.

Preparation: Bring a newspaper, preferably a local paper that the children have seen. Also bring poster board and a marker.

Before the service, write "The Galilean Daily News" across the top of the poster board. Under that write the date: "A.D. 30."

Jesus Feeds 5000

I'd like to talk today about newspapers. Do you or your mom or dad ever look at a newspaper? Do you know what my favorite part of the paper is? That's right, the comics.

I thought we'd talk about how a newspaper works. (*Hold up the paper.*) This is our local paper. Across the top is the name of the paper (*read it*) and here in big print is the headline. The headline tells us the most important news of the day. On this day the headline reads: New Shopping Center Coming to Town. And then under the headline is the story that tells us all about the new shopping center that is coming.

There are other articles here on the front. They have smaller headlines. These articles are important but not as important as the one with the headline at the top of the page. That's the way a newspaper works. And of course there are some pictures in the newspaper here, too.

I thought we'd write our own newspaper today. Do you think we can do that? Great! I'd like to write a newspaper article about the story in today's Gospel. Let's pretend that we live in ancient Galilee back when Jesus lived. Let's pretend that it is the day that Jesus did the miracle we read about in today's Gospel reading. We're going to report about that in our paper.

Do you remember what happened in the Gospel reading? Let

me quickly go over the story. Then we'll write a newspaper article about it.

Jesus was on the shore of the Sea of Galilee. More than 5000 people came to hear him. That's a lot of people, isn't it? (*Compare it to some nearby city of similar size.*) Jesus wanted to feed the people, and the disciples didn't have any food. But somebody in the crowd had some food. Do you remember who that was? (*Be prepared to answer this because the children may not be able to: a boy.*)

That's right. There was a boy in the crowd who had some food. He had five loaves of bread and two fish. It wasn't very much food. It surely wasn't enough to feed a large crowd!

But the boy gave his five loaves and two fish to Jesus. Jesus prayed and thanked God for the food. Then what did Jesus do? (*Jesus fed the people.*)

That's right. Jesus fed all the people. He made a miracle. Using that little bit of food, he fed over 5000 people. In fact the Bible says that after everyone had eaten, there were twelve baskets of food left over—more than they had started with. What a great miracle Jesus did!

Well, let's see if we can report this in our newspaper. (Hold up the poster board.) This will be the front page of our paper. I decided to call our newspaper *The Galilean Daily News* since Jesus was by the Sea of Galilee when he did this miracle. What should we put for the main headline on our paper? What is the most important news? (*Jesus Feeds 5000. Affirm other responses as well. Suggest that they could be other stories.*)

That would be a great headline. (Write "Jesus Feeds 5000" across the top of the poster board.) Of course then under our headline we'd have to write the story of all that Jesus did. Let's draw some lines to represent our story.

What other things should we put on our front page? (*Give the children a chance to think. Use other responses, such as "Boy gives five loaves and two fish," "Leftovers Collected," "Jesus Blesses Bread," "People Amazed by Jesus" and so on.*)

Do you know what else our newspaper needs? It needs a picture. What should we have a picture of? (*Bread, fish, Jesus feeding the people.*)

I'm not a very good artist, but let's draw a picture here. (*Draw a box for the picture, then draw a quick picture.*) Let's pretend that's a picture of Jesus feeding the people.

Let's write one more news story across the bottom here. How about "People Believe Jesus Is Savior." (*Write that across the bottom.*)

Let's look at our newspaper. (*Hold up the paper for the children to see.*) What do you think? I think it's great! Our paper tells us that Jesus took care of people. He fed more than 5000 people at one time. And our newspaper helps us to remember that Jesus is our Savior. Those are important things for us to know. Jesus takes care of people. Jesus is the Savior.

Just as our newspaper tells us the news, we are to tell others the good news that Jesus always loves us and always cares for us. That really is good news!   **—M.B.**

Eleventh Sunday after Pentecost

————————————— • —————————————

The Gospel: John 6:24-39

Focus: Jesus is the one who has come from heaven to be the Savior of the world.

Experience: Show the children a globe and talk about the world. Then talk about how Jesus loves people all around the world.

Preparation: Bring a world globe.

The Whole World

I brought a globe with me today. (*Show the children the globe.*) What does a globe show us? (*The world, countries, continents, where we are.*)

That's right. A globe shows us the world. And all the different colors show us different countries. Each color is a different country. There sure are a lot of countries in the world. Here is the United States. Here is Mexico. Here is Canada. (*Point to the various countries.*) Over here is China. Here is Australia.

There are many countries in the world. Each country has many people. It's a big world we live in.

Let me ask you a question. Where in this world of ours are the people that Jesus loves? If you look at the globe, where on it are the people that Jesus cares about? (*The children may or may not be able to answer this. Be prepared either way.*)

Does Jesus love the people in the United States? (*Point to the U.S.A. Yes.*) How about Mexico? Does Jesus love the people in Mexico? (*Point to Mexico. Yes.*)

Let's find China again. (*Point to China.*) Does Jesus love the people in China? (*Yes.*)

Of course. Jesus loves all people all across the globe. In fact today's Gospel reading tells us that. It says that Jesus came down from heaven to give life to all the world. The wonderful news is that Jesus loves the whole world and all the people in it. There are many people and many countries. And Jesus cares for us all.

That means that we Christians have a job to do. There are people in many places of the world that don't know about Jesus and his love. We as Christians are to tell them about Jesus because Jesus wants everyone to know his care.

But the good news for us to remember today is that Jesus loves all people all around the world. There are many countries and many people. Jesus loves us all. He wants you and me and all people to share in his family.

(If your group enjoys singing, you could close by singing together "He's Got the Whole World in His Hands.")   **—M.B.**

Twelfth Sunday after Pentecost
———————————— • ————————————

The Gospel: John 6:41-51

Focus: Today's Gospel proclaims that Jesus is the bread of life. This sermon explores how Jesus is our friend who cares for us in all of life.

Experience: Talk with the children about Jesus being our friend.

What a Friend!

I'd like to talk with you about a friend today. How many of you have friends? (*Have the children raise their hands.*) That's great! Friends are important. Let me ask you another question. What is a friend? (*Allow time for responses and affirm what is shared.*)

Good. Friends are people that we like and who like us. Friends are people who care about us. Friends are very important. They share with us. They care for us. They make us feel better when we have a bad day. They are happy with us when we have a good day. Do you know what I like most about friends? Friends make me feel special.

Today's Gospel reading tells us about a special friend that we have. His name is Jesus. According to the Bible, Jesus was sent from heaven to be our Savior and our friend. Did you know that Jesus is our friend? (*Yes.*)

He is! He is a very special friend. Jesus cares for us in all of life. He makes us feel better when we have a bad day. He is happy with us when we have a good day. In his love he makes us special. There is nobody more important than Jesus, and he is a friend for you and me.

There is something that we often do with friends. We talk with them. Do you talk with your friends? (*Allow responses.*) Do you talk with your friends a lot? (*Allow responses.*) I do too. I like to talk with my friends. I spend a lot of time doing that. We can talk with Jesus too. He is our friend, and he wants us to talk with him. We have a special name for talking to Jesus. Do you know what we call it when we talk to Jesus? (*Praying.*) That's right! We pray. That's what prayer is. Prayer is talking with a friend—our friend Jesus. Let's take some time right now and talk to Jesus. Please fold your hands and close your eyes.

Jesus, thank you for being our friend. Thank you for coming from heaven to be with us and give us life. Help us to know that you will always be with us and will always care for us. Help us to know what a special friend we have in you. Amen.

This week remember that we have a very special friend. He came from heaven to care for us, and he loves each one of us. His name is Jesus.

(You might follow this sermon by having the children and congregation sing together "What a Friend We Have in Jesus.")   **—M.B.**

Thirteenth Sunday after Pentecost
————————————————————•————————————————————

The Gospel: John 6:51-58

Focus: Jesus is the living bread. He gives us all we need because he loves us, not because we deserve it.

Experience: The children will talk about bread and use a children's story to think about bread as a gift of life.

Preparation: Become familiar with the children's story, "The Little Red Hen." You could bring a copy of the story if you prefer to read the story instead of telling it. Also bring a bun or slice of bread in a bag. If today's service is one with Holy Communion, you could show the communion bread as an example.

Bread of Life

Today we're going to talk a little about bread. How many of you like to eat bread? (*Allow responses.*) Bread is good to eat, and it is good for us too. It fills us up and gives us strength.

I know a story about bread. It's called "The Little Red Hen." Do you know the story? (*Allow for responses.*) Well, the story goes like this:

(*You will need to decide how best to tell the story. If your group is fairly outgoing, the children could help tell the story by speaking the parts of the pig, the duck, the cat, and the dog. If you like to tell stories, you can tell the story using your own voice for the various parts. If your group is small enough, you could read the story from a book and show the pictures to the group.*)

Once upon a time there was a little red hen. One day as she was scratching for breakfast for her chicks and herself, she found some wheat seeds.

"Who will help me plant this wheat?" she asked.

"Not I," said the pig.

"Not I," said the duck.

"Not I," said the cat.

"Not I," said the dog. (*These are the standard responses after each question raised by the little red hen.*)

"Then I will plant the wheat myself," said the little red hen. And she did.

The sun shone, the rain fell, and the wheat grew. After many days, it was ready to cut. "Who will help me cut the wheat?" asked the little red hen.

(*Give standard animal responses.*)

"Then I will cut the wheat myself," said the little red hen. And she did.

Next the wheat needed to be ground into flour. "Who will help me carry the wheat to the miller?" asked the little red hen.

(*Give standard animal responses.*)

"Then I will carry the wheat myself," said the little red hen. And she did.

When the flour was ready, it needed to be made into bread and baked. "Who will help me make the bread?" asked the little red hen.

(*Give standard animal responses.*)

"Then I will make the bread myself," said the little red hen. And she did.

When the bread had baked, the little red hen took it out of the oven. "The bread is ready, light and sweet," she said. "Now, who will come and help me eat?"

"I will!" said the pig.

"I will!" said the duck.

"I will!" said the cat.

"I will!" said the dog.

But the little red hen said, "You did not help me plant the wheat. You did not help me cut the wheat. You did not help me carry the wheat. You did not help me bake the bread. And now you will not help me eat. My little chicks and I will eat the bread." And they did.

What do you think about that story? (*Allow for responses.*) Was it sort of mean that the little red hen would only share her bread with her chicks? (*Yes.*) Was it sort of mean that the pig, the duck, the cat, and the dog would never help when the little red hen asked for help? (*Yes.*) Did the pig, the duck, the cat, and the dog *deserve* any bread if they never helped out? (*No. Some children may want to discuss this a bit, but keep the focus on deserving.*) They didn't deserve any bread, and she didn't give them any.

In today's Bible story Jesus said, "I am the living bread that came down from heaven." Why did he say that he was like bread? (*Allow reponses. If the children are puzzled, encourage them by reminding them about the good things about bread: it tastes good, it fills us up, it gives us strength.*) Just like the pig, the duck, the cat, and the dog, we haven't done anything to deserve this bread that Jesus gives. But is Jesus like the little red hen? (*No.*) No, he isn't. Even though we may do many loving and helpful things, we can never do enough to deserve Jesus' love. We don't have to do anything. Jesus loves us because he chooses to, not because we deserve it. Jesus loves us and gives us all we need to live.

(*Hold up your bread.*) Have you noticed that sometimes during church we have bread on the altar? (*Responses.*) We call this Holy Communion. The bread of Holy Communion reminds us that Jesus loves us, not because we deserve it but because he chooses to love us.

I am glad that Jesus is not like the little red hen in our story. I am so thankful that Jesus loves me, and I know that Jesus loves each one of you too! The next time you see bread, remember that Jesus is the living bread from heaven. And remember, Jesus is with you always.   **—L.R.**

Fourteenth Sunday after Pentecost

———————————— • ————————————

The Gospel: John 6:60-69

Focus: Jesus is the Holy Son of God.

Experience: The children will state their belief in Jesus just as Peter did in the Gospel. They will recall the things Jesus did that show he is God's Son. They will consider telling others about Jesus.

Preparation: Bring a picture of Jesus.

Who Is This Man?

(*Hold up the picture of Jesus.*) Do you know who this is? (*Allow responses.*) Yes, you are right, it is Jesus. Do you know what makes Jesus very special? (*Allow responses.*) In today's Gospel, Jesus' friend Peter put it this way: "We have come to believe and know that you are the Holy One of God." What did Peter mean by that? (*This is not an easy question. Allow responses and help them express their ideas.*) Peter said he knew that Jesus was very special and that he believed that Jesus was sent by God. I believe these things about Jesus. Do you? (*Allow responses.*) What do you know about Jesus that shows you he was the Holy One of God? (*Allow responses.*)

Peter knew some of these things too. How did Peter know about Jesus? (*Peter was there with Jesus for many of the special things that Jesus did.*) That's right, but that was a long time ago. You weren't there, and I wasn't there either. Yet we all said earlier that we believe Jesus is the Holy One of God, just as Peter said. We didn't see Jesus do these things, so how can we believe?

(*We learn about Jesus at church, in Sunday school, and at home. We learn and we believe, we listen and we believe, and we tell other people about Jesus and sometimes they believe too.*) That's right.

Did you ever tell someone about Jesus? (*Allow responses.*) Sometime you might have the chance to do that. And then maybe someone else will know and believe that Jesus is the Holy One of God — just like Peter believed, just like I believe, and just like you believe in him too.

How can we help someone else to know and believe in Jesus? (*Allow responses. We can talk to them, pray, write, invite a friend to come to church with us, sing or play music, and other ways.*) Why don't you think about that this week? Let's all do what we can to share the good news that Jesus loves us.   **—S.L.**

Fifteenth Sunday after Pentecost

The Gospel: Mark 7:1-8, 14-15, 21-23

Focus: God wants us to truly honor him, not just make empty promises.

Experience: The children will talk about the difference between making a promise and keeping it.

Promises, Promises

How many of you have ever played on a teeter-totter? (*The children may be more familiar with the word* seesaw.) It's fun to play on a tee-ter-totter! When I was little, my friend and I used to play a game on the teeter-totter called "Farmer Brown." Have you ever played it? (*Allow responses.*) It goes like this:

When you ride the teeter-totter, sometimes you're up and some-times you're down, right? When I would get down, I would try to keep my seat down and touching the ground so that my friend would be stuck up in the air.

Then my friend would say, "Farmer Brown, let me down!" And I would say, "If I do, what will you give me?" Then my friend would try to think of what I would really like and would promise to give it to me. For example, he would say, "I'll give you all the spot-ted horses in the world," or "I'll give you a hundred dollars."

Now, we didn't really mean those things. It was just a game. I just imagined all the things I would like to have, and I kept my friend up in the air until she promised me all the things I loved best!

If you were playing that game, what would you want someone to promise you? (*Allow and affirm responses.*) Would you really expect to get what you were promised? (*No.*) These are what people call empty promises—promises that someone makes but never intends to keep.

In the Bible story today, Jesus talks about some people like that. Jesus said the people were hypocrites. Do you know what that means? (*Someone who says they will do one thing and then does some-thing else instead.*)

Jesus said, "This people honors me with their lips, but their hearts are far from me."

The people said they were following God and obeying God's laws, but they had forgotten something very important. They were making empty promises. They had forgotten that the most important thing is to love God with all your heart, all your soul, all your mind, and all your strength.

Sometimes we make empty promises too. Our parents might ask us to do something, and we say "Sure." But then we forget about it and don't do what they asked. Do you know what I mean about empty promises? (*If some are still confused, remind them that an empty promise is a promise we make but don't keep.*)

We may make empty promises, or someone may make empty promises to us, but there is someone who never makes empty promises. Do you know who that is? (*God.*) That's right! And what are some promises God has made to us? (*To love us, care for us, always be with us, give us what we need, protect us, save us.*) God has promised these things to us, and God will always keep his promises.

Jesus asks us to make a promise too. He asks us not to make empty promises to God but to love God with all our hearts. Keep God's love in your heart this week.   **—L.R.**

Sixteenth Sunday after Pentecost

—————————————— • ——————————————

The Gospel: Mark 7:31-37

Focus: Sometimes it is very hard to keep good news to ourselves.

Experience: The children will hear the Bible story and think about times when they have had a hard time keeping a secret.

The Secret That's Hard to Keep

I have a secret! Do you want to know what it is? (*Allow responses.*) OK. This is it—but wait a minute. If I tell you my secret, then it won't be a secret anymore, will it? (*No.*) Oh, now I don't know what to do. (*Show some anguish. Make the children believe that you really want to tell your secret but that you don't know if you should.*) I'm so excited that I want to tell someone about it. If I tell you all quietly, will you promise not to tell anyone else? (*Allow responses.*) OK. This is it. Oh, wait a minute. I just know I shouldn't. If I tell even one person, it won't be a secret anymore. I know. How about if I give you three guesses? If you can guess my secret, then I won't excatly be telling you, right? Let's try it. I'll give *you* three guesses (*point to one child and then another*), and *you* three guesses, and *you* three guesses. Oh, I don't know. Even if I didn't exactly tell you and you just happend to guess, it wouldn't be a secret anymore, would it? (*No.*) That's really hard. This is such a great secret. It's hard to keep a great secret like this one!

Now I will tell you that I have been just pretending to have a secret, but I wanted you to remember how it feels. Have you ever had to keep a secret? (*Allow and affirm responses.*) Was it hard for you to do? (*Responses.*) It's hard to keep quiet about a really good secret, isn't it?

In today's Bible story, Jesus asked a man to keep some good news a secret. The man had trouble talking, and he couldn't hear. When Jesus met the man, he took him away from the crowd and healed the man in private. When the man returned, he could hear again and speak plainly. Jesus asked the people who had seen the miracle to keep it a secret. But the people were amazed. They said, "He has done everything well; he even makes the deaf to hear and the mute to speak." And the more Jesus asked them to keep the secret to themselves, the more they talked about it.

Jesus wasn't angry, but he didn't want people to talk about the miracle. Why do you think he felt that way? (*Affirm their responses.*) We don't know all the reasons, but Jesus did not want his healing miracles to become like tricks that made people believe in him. He healed people because he loved them, not so that they would brag about his great works.

But if you had been the man who was healed, could you have kept the secret? (*No.*) Good news like that is hard to keep to yourself. And Jesus does want us to tell others about him. What can we tell others about Jesus? (*Affirm responses.*) Yes. We can tell them all those things, and most important, we can tell them that Jesus loves them!   **—L.R.**

Seventeenth Sunday after Pentecost

————————————— • —————————————

The Gospel: Mark 8:27-35

Focus: Jesus is the Messiah.

Experience: The children will talk about the question, "Who do you think I am?"

Preparation: You may use the information in the sermon text or replace it with your own. Think about your own life and instances in which people have told you, "You look just like your mother," or "You remind me of . . . " and so on.

Who Do You Think I Am?

When I was your age, my dad's family used to have lots of picnics. The thing I remember best was that people would always try to figure out which family I belonged to. When they found out, they would say, "You sure look like your dad!"

I didn't really think I looked like my dad, but they thought I did. He wore glasses and had gray hair. He was much taller than I was, and his laugh didn't sound like mine. But they could see something I couldn't. I reminded them of him.

Has anyone ever told you that you remind them of someone else? (*Allow and affirm responses.*) How does that make you feel? (*Allow and affirm responses.*) Sometimes that can make us feel good because we may like being compared to someone we admire. But sometimes we might think "That's not me. I'm different than that!"

In today's Bible story, Jesus asked his disciples, "Who do people say that I am?" Do you remember what his disciples told him? (*John the Baptist, Elijah, one of the prophets.*) Why do you think they said that? Do you think Jesus looked like those other men? (*No. But people probably heard about the things Jesus was doing and those things reminded them of stories they had heard about John or Elijah.*)

Then Jesus asked Peter a very important question. He said, "But who do you say that I am?" Peter had been with Jesus for quite a while. He had heard Jesus teach and seen him help people. Do you remember what Peter said? (*"You are the Messiah."*) That's right. Peter recognized who Jesus really was. Do you remember what *Messiah* means? (*Allow for responses but if no one volunteers, help them to define the word.*) It means that Jesus is the one God promised to send—the one who will love us and save us and show us how to live. Jesus, the Messiah, is our Savior. Jesus, the Messiah, is our friend.

Peter knew who Jesus was, and we know who Jesus is. Now we can help others to know Jesus too.   **—L.R.**

Eighteenth Sunday after Pentecost

—————————— • ——————————

The Gospel: Mark 9:30-37

Focus: To be "great" in God's kingdom means that we are willing to serve others.

Experience: The chidren will compare and contrast "greatness" in different areas with what Jesus meant by "greatness" in today's Gospel.

Preparation: Bring in some kind of ribbon or trophy. If you don't have one, make a blue ribbon out of construction paper.

The Greatest

What does it mean to be great? (*Allow for responses.*) Are any of you great at anything? (*Responses.*) What are some things you are great at? (*Affirm responses. They could include sports, music, games, school, or more general things like helping, sharing, and so on.*) Did any of you ever win a prize for doing something well? (*Allow responses and then share your ribbon or trophy and explain what you or someone else did to get it. If you use the construction paper one, say that sometimes schools give out paper prizes like this one for certain contests.*) It's a good feeling to be the greatest and win a prize, isn't it?

Did any of you ever *want* to win a tournament or a contest, but you didn't win? Can you tell us about that? (*Allow responses.*) You might have felt disappointed, but hopefully you had a good time trying and you did your very best.

In today's Gospel, Jesus' friends were talking about being the greatest. They weren't talking about being the greatest runner or the greatest speller or anything like that. They were wondering who was the greatest follower of Jesus. Do you know what he said to them? Can you remember? (*Allow responses.*) He said, "Whoever wants to be first must be last of all, and servant of all." That's a little different from what the disciples expected him to say! What do you think he meant by that? (*Allow responses.*) To be first in God's kingdom means you should think of others first and be a servant to them. That's what Jesus did. The entire reason he came to earth was for *us*, not for him. Jesus thought of us first and served us.

Can you think of ways of caring for others or letting them be first? (*Allow responses. Sharing your toys or letting everyone else pick a cookie first at snack time is a good way.*) That's right.

But when we are busy putting other people first, does that mean that somehow we don't count? (*No.*) The most wonderful thing about God's kingdom is that we can *all* be the greatest! God loves each and every one of us: (*point to children*) you, and you, and you, and you, and all of you, and me, and everyone!   **—S.L.**

Nineteenth Sunday after Pentecost

──────────────────●──────────────────

The Gospel: Mark 9:38-50

Focus: We can learn from others, and they can learn from us.

Experience: The children will learn a simple hand clapping pattern by following the leader's example. The point will be made that children learn by watching others and can be good examples to others.

Preparation: Think of a pattern of five or six hand movements, such as: clap twice, slap your lap twice, slap the floor once, clap once, slap the floor once, and clap once. Learn the pattern.

How Do We Learn?

I'd like to teach you a little game. See if you can do what I do. (*Clap twice.*) You try it! (*They do it.*) Now do this. (*Clap twice slap your lap twice.*) Very good! This time it will be a little harder. (*Clap twice, slap your lap twice, slap the floor once. Continue to teach the children the entire pattern.*)

That's it! You did a good job learning that pattern! How did you learn it? (*Allow responses.*) Yes. You learned it by watching me do it. If I would have said, "Clap your hands," but done something else, that would have mixed you up, wouldn't it? You learned because *I* showed you what I wanted *you* to do. I showed an example.

That's the way children learn a lot of things. They watch grown-ups or older children doing something, and then they try it too. Can you think of some things you learned to do just by watching other people? Think of things that you weren't really taught, things you just watched and then did. (*Allow responses.*) How about talking and walking? Or giving a hug. Babies get hugs, and then they know how to give hugs.

Some of you may have learned the Lord's Prayer this way. Nobody had to teach it to you, but you heard it often, and after a while, you knew it too. You learned by following an example.

Do any of you have little brothers or sisters or maybe younger neighbors or cousins? Did you know that they learn from you? Can anyone give an example of this? (*Allow time for responses and affirm what is shared. If no one volunteers, simply continue.*) I've known families where a little brother picks up his big brother's baseball bat and tries to swing it. And sometimes little sisters know all the words to a big sister's Brownie song. Has that happened to any of you? (*Allow responses.*)

In today's Gospel Jesus talks about teaching others. He wants us to be good examples of how to love and care for other people.

When other children see you sharing your toys, you are teaching them to share. In church when you sing the hymns and say the responses, you are teaching other children what to do in church. So sometimes you are a teacher! What other good things can you do at home or at church to teach others? (*Allow responses.*) Good suggestions! We learn by watching others, and others learn by watching us, so let's remember to teach good lessons!   —**S.L.**

Twentieth Sunday after Pentecost

───────────────── • ─────────────────

The Gospel: Mark 10:2-16

Focus: Children are important to Jesus, and Jesus is important to children.

Experience: The children will list all the things their church does for children and thank the people who have helped them learn about Jesus.

Preparation: Bring a marker and a piece of poster board.

Jesus Loves the Little Children

Today's Gospel reminded me of a few songs: "Jesus Loves the Little Children," "Jesus Loves Me," and "Children of the Heavenly Father." Can any of you think why? (*Allow responses.*) Yes. Jesus loves children! The disciples thought Jesus was too busy to bother with children, but they were wrong about that. Jesus enjoys children very much, and the Bible tells us he was happy to spend time with children.

Children are very important at our church too. Do you know that? (*Allow responses.*) Can you think of things our church does for children? I'm going to write down all the things you can think of. (*Allow responses and comment accordingly. This will vary from church to church. As the children speak, make a list of the various activities such as Sunday school, choir, VBS, and so on.*) That's quite a list!

You know, these activities don't just happen on their own. Let's go back over the list and write down the names of the people who make each activity possible. (*Allow the children to say the names as you write them down.*) Wow! That's a lot of names. It takes a lot of time to do all these things. Why do these people do them? (*Allow responses.*) They believe that it is important for children to know and love Jesus. Many of them first knew Jesus when they were children, and they want to share Jesus' love with you.

Can you imagine how your life would be different if you didn't know anything about Jesus? Can you tell me some ways it would be different? (*Allow responses.*) That's right. There would be no one to pray to. When you felt lonely and scared, you wouldn't know that Jesus was right there with you. You wouldn't know anything about the wonderful joy of Jesus' birth at Christmas and his rising again at Easter. You would have no idea that God loved you so much that he sent his son to die for you and then to rise again. Your life would really be different. It would be kind of empty. So let's take a minute to thank all these people who give their time and effort to bring you closer to Jesus. I'll read off the list of names, and when I'm all done, let's all give these people a great big round of applause! (*Read the list and start the applause.*)   **—S.L.**

Twenty-first Sunday after Pentecost
———————————— • ————————————

The Gospel: Mark 10:17-27 (28-30)

Focus: Those who have much should help those who have little.

Experience: The children will discuss what it would be like to be rich. They will say all the things they would do if they had a lot of money. The Gospel will be reviewed after they imagine what a poor person would do if he or she were given some money. At the end of the sermon each child will receive a penny or other coin to put in the offering plate later in the service.

Preparation: Bring a roll of pennies (fifty cents) or a roll of other coins.

Something to Give

Do you know what it means to be rich? (*Allow responses.*) That's right. It means having a lot of money. Let's imagine for just a minute that each of you is rich. Suppose that you have lots and lots of money at home and you can do anything with it that you would like to do. What would you do with it? (*Allow responses.*) Those ideas sound like a lot of fun! I wouldn't mind doing some of those things myself.

Now. Let's use our imaginations again. Let's imagine that we are very, very poor. What does it mean to be poor? (*Allow responses.*) That's right. Poor people don't have enough money. Poor people are the opposite of rich people. If you were very poor and someone gave you some money, what do you think you might do with it? (*Allow responses.*) That's right. Because poor people don't have much money, the money they do get has to go to pay for the things they really need, like food.

When we pretended to be rich, we talked about things we would like to have. We didn't really need those things. We just wanted them. We can get along fine without these things, can't we? (*Allow responses.*) But poor people sometimes have to go without things they really do need, and that can be very difficult. Have you ever gone all day without any food? Have you ever gone to sleep on a bench in a park because you didn't have a house? How do you think it feels to be very sick and not be able to go to the doctor because you have no money? (*Allow responses.*)

What could rich people do to help out the poor people? (*Allow responses. They could share some of their money or clothes or help a poor person to get a job or find a place to live.*) Did you know that our church helps poor people? (*Give specific examples of what your church does.*)

Today's Gospel is about a man who was very rich. Jesus told this man that he should give his money to the poor. Who can tell me what the man did? (*Allow responses.*) If you had some money, what would you do with it? Would you like to share it with some poor people? (*Allow responses.*)

Well, guess what I have in my pocket. (*Hold up the roll of pennies or other coins and break it open, letting the pennies or coins fall on the floor in a pile.*) We are going to divide up these pennies, and you may take your money back to your seat with you. You will be rich, just like the man in the Gospel! But you said if you were rich, you'd give money to help poor people. Now you can do that. You can take your penny(ies) and put it (them) in the offering plate so that they will go through our church to help some poor people. And next week you can bring your own money to put in the offering plate. Jesus doesn't tell us how much to give. You can give one of your coins, some of your money, or all of your money. The only thing Jesus asks us to do is give joyfully.

(*Divide up the pennies.*) Now you each have some pennies. Now you are rich! Please don't forget what Jesus said rich people should do with their money—help others!   **—S.L.**

Twenty-second Sunday after Pentecost
— • —

The Gospel: Mark 10:35-45

Focus: The measure of greatness in the kingdom of God depends not upon what we do for ourselves but rather upon what we are willing to do for others. In love we are to serve one another.

Experience: First establish a focus of measuring using a yardstick, set of scales, and measuring cup. Then discuss how we measure greatness in a baseball player, a president or other leader, a business person, and finally a Christian.

Preparation: Bring a ruler or yardstick, a bathroom scale, a measuring cup, a baseball card, and a picture of the President of the United States (for Canada, a picture of the Prime Minister).

A Measure of Greatness

This morning I have brought with me some objects that I think you will all recognize. First, we will identify them, and then we will see if we can determine what they all have in common. (*Show them the ruler, ask them what it is, and then ask what it is used for. Do the same with the bathroom scale and the measuring cup.*) These are all items that are used for what? (*Allow responses.*) That is correct. These tools are all used to measure different objects—how long, how heavy, and how much.

Did you know that we sometimes use different ways of measuring to determine how good, important, or successful a person is at something that they do? For example, I have here a baseball card with the picture of a major league baseball player on it. I can't tell how good or successful at baseball this player is, though, by just looking at his picture. What else do I need? (*Allow responses.*) I need to flip the card over and look at the records on the back of the card. By looking at his batting average, how many home runs he has hit, and so on, I can tell how good he really is at baseball.

Who can tell me who this person is? (*Hold up a picture of the President of the United States or Prime Minister of Canada.*) That is correct. President (Prime Minister) _____. Would you say this man is important? Certainly, the person who is President (Prime Minister) has a very important job. Just like the baseball player, however, how good a person is as president (prime minister) will depend on what that person does. A good way to measure greatness is in the next election. If the people think the person is doing a good job, they will probably reelect that person.

In business we usually measure how good someone is by the amount of money that person makes. People who do well usually see their business grow and the amount of money they make increase. So, as you can see, greatness is usually measured by what a person does in a particular area.

What about greatness as a Christian, as a child of God? What measure do we use to determine how great we are as children of God? Christ himself gives us the answer to that question. He says, "Whoever wishes to become great among you must be your servant." Greatness as a child of God does not depend on what we do for ourselves but rather on what we are willing to do for others. So my young friends, serve one another in love, for that is the measure of a true child of God.   **—D.H.**

Twenty-third Sunday after Pentecost

───────────────────── • ─────────────────────

The Gospel: Mark 10:46-52

Focus: Jesus wants us to be persistent in our prayers.

Experience: You and the children will explore the idea of "giving up," which often crosses our minds in the tasks we do, or attempt to do, daily. This is also true as we pray to God. The key to success is to not give up as we ask God for help.

Preparation: Have a trick ready that you are fairly certain none of the children know but one which can easily be taught to one of them in a short time. I have used the "pulling the string through the neck" trick very successfully. Directions for that trick are:

Take a string that is three feet long and tie the ends together. Place the string over your upturned thumbs and draw the string taut. With the string in that position lift the string over your head, and place both strands of it against the back of your neck. Now bring your open hands together in front of you (as if you were clapping) with thumbs still upright. Do this a few times and each time lower your right hand, so finally you can slip the index finger of your right hand into the loop with your left thumb. When you do so, allow the loop on your right thumb to slide off. As you bring your hands quickly apart, the string will slide over your left shoulder but will appear to have passed through your neck.

Keep on Praying!

This morning I would like to begin by showing all of you a trick. Before I do the trick, however, I need one of you to volunteer to do the same trick right after I am finished. Do I have a volunteer? (*Choose an older child and ask him or her to come forward. Do the trick you have selected, and as soon as you have finished, allow the volunteer to try two or three times to do the trick and then continue.*) You appear to be having some difficulty doing the trick I showed you. Why? (*The child will most likely say that it is too difficult.*) I really appreciate your willingness to try this. You worked so hard to make the trick work even though you didn't succeed. I have a young friend who is going to take you aside and teach the trick to you right now. (*Send your volunteer off with your assistant to learn the trick.*)

In our daily lives we face problems. As we work through those problems, we learn and grow. It is a good feeling to be able to figure out and solve a problem. There are times, however, when the problem is so difficult or so big that we feel like giving up. At times like that it is so good to know that we have a God who loves us and a Savior who has promised always to be with us.

In our Gospel lesson for today we heard the story of blind Bartimaeus. Jesus gave to Bartimaeus what no one else could—the ability to see. It wasn't easy, however, for Bartimaeus to get to Jesus. When he shouted out, "Jesus, Son of David, have mercy on me!" the crowd warned him to be quiet. Did that stop Bartimaeus? No, indeed! He shouted even louder because he believed in Jesus and wasn't going to give up easily. His shout was a prayer to Jesus for help. Jesus answered his prayer and granted him his sight. Why? Bartimaeus believed and refused to give up. As we lift our prayers to God in Jesus' name, let us remember not to give up if we don't get an answer right away. Like Bartimaeus we should keep on praying because we know our God is faithful.

Why don't we check with our volunteer and see how he (she) is coming with that trick. (*Have the volunteer demonstrate mastery of the trick.*) Remember my young friends, don't give up.   **—D.H.**

Twenty-fourth Sunday after Pentecost

The Gospel: Mark 12:28-34 (35-37)

Focus: In his earthly ministry Jesus repeatedly stressed the importance of love for God and love for our neighbor.

Experience: The children will talk about rules they use and compare these to Jesus' most important rule: love God.

Preparation: Bring the following items: a list of rules from a school, a driver's manual, a rule book for baseball or some other sport, and a Bible.

The Greatest Commandment

A few days ago I was in a kindergarten classroom and on the wall I saw a list. Let me tell you some of the items that were on the list, and see if you can figure out what kind of list it was. (*Read the following statements from the list: we walk in the classroom; we keep our hands to ourselves; we listen to the teacher and to others; we talk quietly; we take good care of our toys and books.*) What kind of a list do you think I was reading? (*Allow responses.*) You are right! That was a list of the rules for the classroom. What do rules tell us? (*Allow responses.*) Yes, rules let everyone know what they can and cannot do in a certain place or situation. It would be very difficult to get anything done in a classroom if all the students did whatever they pleased. Rules provide us with the order we need to keep everyone safe and to complete our work.

Is school the only place we find rules? (*Allow responses.*) No, of course not. Rules can be found in many other areas of our lives. Today I have with me some "rule books" that people use for specific activities (*Show the children a driver's manual.*) Here is the first one. When young people are preparing to get a driver's license, this rule book is very important. It contains all the rules for driving and, as you can see, there are many of them. Of all the rules for driving, which rule is more important than all the others? (*Pause and consider a few responses.*) That is a very difficult question, isn't it?

How many of you play team sports? (*Allow responses.*) Every sport you participate in has a set of rules. Here is a rule book for (*whatever sport you choose*). Just look at the size of the book. Of all of these rules for playing (*the sport you have chosen*), which rule is the most important of all? (*Pause for responses.*) There are so many rules that it is difficult to pick out just one and say that is more important than all the others.

(*Hold up the Bible and ask the children to identify it.*) As God's children, we use this book to learn about God's will for us. We want to know what behavior is pleasing to God and what behavior is not. Like the other books I showed you, this book has many rules or commandments that are important. Is there one rule or commandment, however, that is more important than all the others?

Fortunately for us, someone asked Jesus that same question many years ago. Jesus didn't hesitate at all in answering it, either. Jesus said, "You shall love the Lord your God with all your heart, and with all your soul, and with all your mind, and with all your strength. You shall love your neighbor as yourself. There is no other commandment greater than these."

It's good for us to remember these helpful words that Jesus told us. The most important thing that a Christian can do is to love — love God, love others, and love ourselves. As Jesus said, "There is no commandment greater than these."   **—D.H.**

Twenty-fifth Sunday after Pentecost

The Gospel: Mark 12:43-44

Focus: The widow gave willingly just as Jesus did when he lived, died, and rose again for our salvation.

Experience: You and the children will talk about what matters most in the giving of a gift. It is not the amount or value of the gift but rather the willingness with which it is given. Willingness is the true measure of generosity.

Preparation: The message is in story form and lends itself to dramatization. Obtain the assistance of older children or youth in acting out the story as you tell it.

Be Willing

Today in our Gospel lesson we heard about people bringing their gifts or offerings of money to God. Jesus watched the people as they did this, and he said something interesting about our giving.

I would like to tell you a story about a boy named Cecil. Cecil was going to celebrate a birthday—his sixth. His mother decided to have a small birthday party to which Cecil could invite three of his best friends.

Cecil knew exactly who he would invite: Claude, Teddy, and Willie. Cecil and these three friends called themselves the "fearsome foursome." They were good buddies and spent a lot of time together. The day of the party each of Cecil's three friends brought a gift for him. Each in turn gave Cecil his gift.

Claude, whom we can call "Clinging Claude," was the first to give Cecil his gift. Claude and Cecil both loved Nintendo, and they would often window shop for the latest games for their machines. Both had their eye on a baseball game. To Claude's amazement his mother bought the baseball game for him to give to Cecil. When Cecil took the brightly wrapped gift from Claude, he almost had to pry it from his hands. In fact, when Claude finally released his grip, Cecil nearly tumbled over backward. Cecil's eyes lit up when he saw the game. Claude looked very pale and near tears.

Next came Teddy. We could call him "Turn-about Teddy." Teddy gave Cecil a very special gift—a football just like the ones the players use in the NFL. When Teddy gave Cecil the gift, he did so with a big smile on his face. He was still smiling five minutes later when he handed Cecil an invitation to his birthday party that was just two weeks away.

Finally, it was Willie's turn to give his gift to Cecil. We could call him "Willing Willie." Willie had thought long and hard about a gift for Cecil. He liked Cecil very much. He finally decided upon the gift he would give his special friend. He gave Cecil a baseball. This wasn't just any baseball. It was a baseball that had been autographed by Jose Canseco. Jose Canseco was Cecil and Willie's favorite player. The baseball belonged to Willie, and it was his prized possession. To give it as a gift was quite an act of friendship. He didn't cling to it and he certainly did not expect it back. He gave it willingly.

Like the widow in our story for today, it wasn't what Willie gave that was important but how it was given. It isn't always easy to be a willing giver. But if we think of all the blessings God has given us, we can give to others joyfully.

May we all be "Willing Willie's" as we share our gifts with others and with our God.   **—D.H.**

Twenty-sixth Sunday after Pentecost

—————————————— • ——————————————

The Gospel: Mark 13:1-13

Focus: As children of God, we must stand firm in our faith.

Experience: The children will be introduced to a new product that doesn't live up to its advertising claims. God's warning to his disciples to "watch out" so that they wouldn't be deceived applies just as much today as it did then.

Preparation: Bring a cereal box that you have covered with aluminum foil, overlaid with a picture of a clown, and titled "Zippety Doo-Dah Cereal." Fill the box with twigs, grass, rocks, and so on. Bring a bowl and spoon as well as a prize which should be placed just inside the box. You will need an older child to ask the *"But what's in it?"* question several times.

Watch Out!

How many of you sometimes eat cereal for breakfast in the morning? There are so many cereals to pick from today that it must be hard to pick out the one you like best.

Well, I am excited today because I have a brand new cereal to show you. The people here this morning will be the first ever to see this new cereal. I have it in this bag, and I think you are going to like it. Enough talk. . . . Let's have a look.

I am pleased to introduce you to "Zippety Doo-Da Cereal!" Just look at this shiny yet colorful box and the clown on the front. It's the best new cereal you can buy. I promise! (*The first time this question is asked, "What's in it?" ignore the question and forge ahead.*) Not only do we have a new cereal here, but we have a jingle to go with it. It goes like this:

> *Zippety Doo-Da, Zippety Ay*
> *Go to the grocery store and buy this today.*
> *Just try one bowlful and we're sure you'll say*
> *Zippety Doo-Da, Zippety Ay.*

(*Again the question is raised, "What's in it?"*) Again the question is dodged, but slyly.

Did you happen to catch the message on the back of the box? Zippety Doo-Da Cereal! Free Prizes Inside! It's a great prize—I promise!

What a deal—a new cereal and prizes as well! Why don't we take a look at the prize. (*Pull out the prize and show it to the children.*) What a great prize! (*The question is asked more emphatically this time: "What's in it?" On this occasion, address yourself to the question.*) What's in it? Well, that's a fair question that deserves a . . . volunteer. Who would like to try this new Zippety Doo-Da Cereal? You'll love it—I promise! (*Use the questioner as your helper as you pour a bowl of grass, twigs, leaves, stones, and whatever else you chose to put in your Zippety Doo-Da Cereal.*)

Would you like milk on your cereal? Sugar? What's wrong? (*Have the volunteer tell the others what's in the cereal.*) I don't know many people who would want this in their cereal bowl in the morning. What I told you about the cereal was quite different from what I actually gave to you! The promises I made were empty promises. They were simply not true. We must be careful so we are not led astray by empty promises and left with nothing.

Jesus warned his disciples to beware of people who would try to lead them astray with empty promises, people who would tell the disciples to follow them and not Jesus. Only by trusting and following Jesus could they have their sins forgiven and receive eternal life.

Jesus had a job for the disciples—to share with everyone the good news of God's love. Jesus wants us to do the same thing today. The job wasn't easy then, and it still isn't easy today. But Jesus tells us we will have help. Jesus sent the Holy Spirit to give us strength and help us know what to say.

I'm sorry about the cereal today. I made some promises that really weren't true. But there is someone who makes promises that are true. Jesus promised to give us the power of the Holy Spirit. And we know that Jesus' promises are true because he loves us.

—D.H.

Twenty-seventh Sunday after Pentecost

———————————— • ————————————

The Gospel: Mark 13:24-31

Focus: Jesus is coming again.

Experience: The children will recall the phrase, "ready or not, here I come," from the game, "Hide and Go Seek." These words can also be applied to the second coming of Jesus Christ. Those who know and love Jesus as their Lord and Savior will rejoice when he returns.

Preparation: Bring a small rubber ball or other object that is used in a game the children play and would know.

Ready or Not, Here I Come

Growing up as a child, I remember many of the fun times I spent with my friends. I still remember some of the games we used to play. The boys liked to play a game with a ball (*show the ball, if you have one*). It was a simple game to understand, but it was not easy to play. One of the bigger boys would throw the ball as high in the air as he could. The object of the game was to catch the ball with your bare hands. Believe me, that wasn't easy.

Another game we played as children was one that I am sure many of you have played as well. Rather than telling you the name of the game I am talking about, let me give you a clue that I think will help you guess what it is. What game uses these words: "Ready or not, here I come"? (*Allow responses.*) That's right! Hide and Go Seek. "Ready or not, here I come" is what the person who is It says just before trying to find everyone who has hidden.

If you have already found a good hiding place, you really don't mind hearing those words. In fact, you look forward to getting the game underway. If on the other hand you're still looking for a place to hide, those words send you into a panic.

It is that way for people when we talk about the second coming of Jesus Christ. Jesus came once as a tiny baby in Bethlehem, and before long we will celebrate his birth with what special holiday? (*Allow responses.*) That's right, Christmas. Many people look forward to that event every year. We sing songs like "Joy to the World" to remember this happy occasion.

But did you know that Jesus is coming again? When he comes again, it won't be as a tiny baby born in humble surroundings. We are told in our Gospel for today that we will "see the Son of Man coming in clouds with great power and glory." Jesus will come as our mighty King. What will Jesus be coming to do? (*Allow responses.*) He will be coming to take his children home to be with him in heaven.

What a wonderful day it will be for those who know and love Jesus as their Lord and Savior. We will be going to our new and glorious home in heaven. While we wait for our Lord to return, we have a job to do. Does anyone know what that might be? (*Allow responses.*) Yes, we need to tell people about Jesus' great love for them. Then they, too, will be ready when he comes again. —**D.H.**

Christ the King—Last Sunday after Pentecost
————————————•————————————

The Gospel: John 18:33-37

Focus: Jesus is the King of kings!

Experience: The children will name job titles after listening to some clues. They will also hear that Jesus was best known for what he did.

Preparation: Talk with some people from your congregation who have easily identified occupations, and ask them to assist you with a game called "Are you a _____?" If you prefer, instead of that, you may read clues about familiar occupations and the children may then guess the occupations.

Are You a King?

As I was walking down the aisle in the grocery store the other day, I met a man with very large muscles in his arms. I greeted him as he approached me. I asked him if he did a certain kind of exercise, and he said yes. What do you think he did to get such large muscles? (*Lifted weights. Affirm other answers.*) It was easy for me to tell by his large muscles that this man lifted weights. Sometimes, however, it isn't easy to tell what people are or do when you first meet them. In our Gospel for today Pilate, the Roman governor, did not recognize Jesus as a king. We will find out why in a few moments, but first I have a guessing game I would like for you to play with me.

The name of the game is "I Know Who You Are." I will read some clues that describe someone's job. When I have finished, you should raise your hand if you know what job I'm talking about.

(*The following two occupations are suggestions only. You should use occupations represented in your congregation. If you wish, describe the jobs of several members of your congregation. Then when their occupation is identified, introduce them by name to the children.*)

People come to see me when they are sick. I tell them what is wrong with them. Sometimes I give them medicine or a shot. (*As children raise their hands, choose one to respond. Then introduce the person to the children.*) Very good.

Let's try another. I wear a uniform when I work. I also wear a badge and carry a gun. It is my job to take people to jail when they have broken the law. (*Choose a child to respond.*) Very good!

Let's try this one. I do my work at a school. It is my job to help students learn when they come to my classroom. My boss is called the principal. (*Response.*) Great! You did a very good job of identifying the work all of these people do.

Remember, I said that in today's Bible story Pilate, the Roman governor, did not recognize Jesus as a king. Why? Did Jesus have a palace to live in? (*No.*) Did Jesus wear a fine robe and a beautiful crown? (*No.*) Did Jesus have a country he ruled over? (*No.*) Jesus had none of the possessions that an earthly king usually has.

Jesus was not the king of a country. He did not have an army. Jesus is the King of love. And just as we recognized the jobs of the people in our congregation because of what they do, we recognize that Jesus is King because of the things he has done. He came to love and serve all people.

We can thank God for sending the Holy Spirit into our hearts and opening our eyes to recognize Jesus as the King of kings. Now each time we tell the story of Jesus' love to another person we help his kingdom to grow.   **—D.H.**